QUEEN OF THE ELEPHANTS

Mark Shand received the Travel Writer of the Year Award for his number one bestseller *Travels on my Elephant*. His previous book, *Skulduggery*, with photographs by Don McCullin, is the story of his search for the head-hunting tribes of Indonesia. He wrote the script and narrated the 'Discovery' feature-length television film 'Queen of the Elephants'.

Mark Shand

QUEEN OF THE ELEPHANTS

WITH PHOTOGRAPHS BY
Aditya Patankar

VINTAGE

Published by Vintage 1996

2 4 6 8 10 9 7 5 3 1

Copyright © Mark Shand 1995

The right of Mark Shand to be identified as the author of
this work has been asserted by him in accordance with
the Copyright, Designs and Patents Act, 1988

First published in Great Britain by
Jonathan Cape Ltd, 1995

Vintage
Random House, 20 Vauxhall Bridge Road, London SW1V 2SA

Random House Australia (Pty) Limited
20 Alfred Street, Milsons Point, Sydney
New South Wales 2061, Australia

Random House New Zealand Limited
18 Poland Road, Glenfield,
Auckland 10, New Zealand

Random House South Africa (Pty) Limited
PO Box 337, Bergvlei, South Africa

Random House UK Limited Reg. No. 954009

A CIP catalogue record for this book
is available from the British Library

ISBN 0 09 959201 0

Papers used by Random House UK Ltd are natural, recy-
clable products made from wood grown in sustainable
forests. The manufacturing processes conform to
the environmental regulations of the country of origin

Printed and bound in Great Britain by
Cox & Wyman, Reading, Berkshire

for my mother
Rosalind Shand
and my friend
Andrew Fraser

Contents

There is a mystery behind that masked grey visage, an ancient life force, delicate and mighty, awesome and enchanted, commanding the silence ordinarily reserved for mountain peaks, great fires, and the sea.

Peter Matthiessen

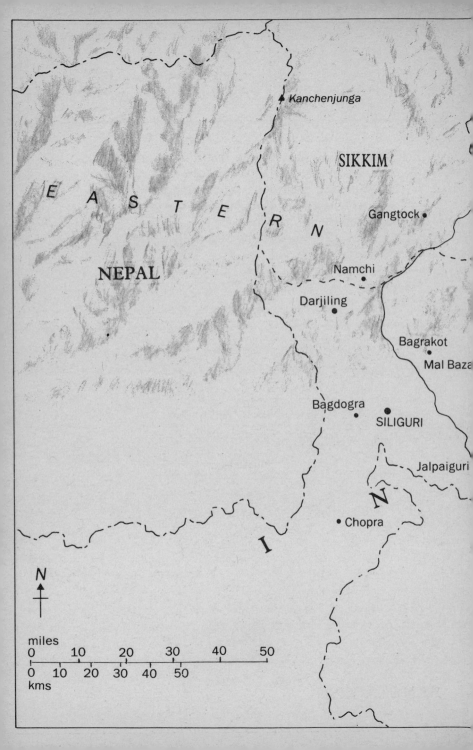

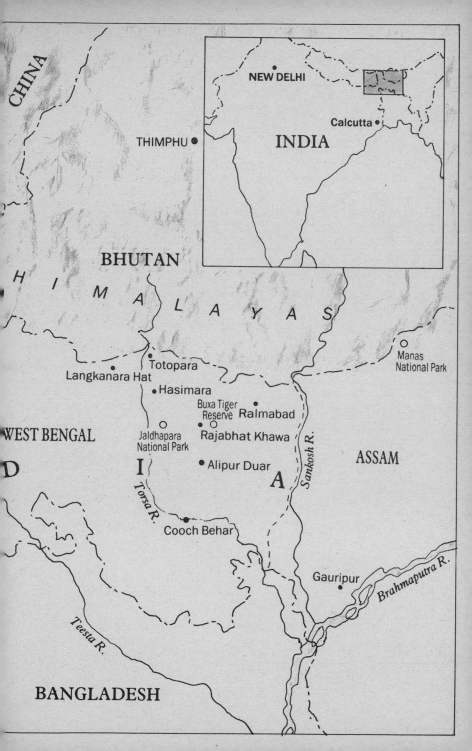

Prologue

'You really think she'll recognise me?' I asked Aditya anxiously for the umpteenth time.

I was back in India with my old friend, the photographer and Maratha nobleman, Aditya Patankar.

A few years ago, on a whim, I had decided to buy an elephant and ride it across India. After weeks of searching for available elephants in the state of Orissa in eastern India, Aditya and I had finally stumbled across a scrawny ill-treated female elephant being used for begging by a bunch of unscrupulous mendicants who were passing themselves off as holy men. It was love at first sight, and after a series of complex negotiations she became mine. I named her Tara.

We were joined by four eccentric minders, including a drunken mahout called Bhim and an ex-taxi driver, who were all soon captivated by Tara's charms, and we meandered slowly northwards across country like a small rag-tag army, towards the great elephant fair at Sonepur in the state of Bihar. There, reluctantly, I intended to sell her, but happily, at the last moment, Tara was rescued, and she is now cared for by friends of mine in India.

Since then, life has not treated Aditya so well. The familiar loping gait that I remembered from those days on the road was now just a distant memory. A year after our journey he was knocked off his motorcycle by one of Delhi's notorious killer buses and dragged a hundred yards along the road, entangled in the chassis. The femur of his left leg was shattered. There followed months of painful treatment, during which an ill-fitting prosthesis was inserted into his leg, followed by somewhat inefficient physiotherapy. He finally emerged, battered, scarred, and virtually a cripple.

But Marathas are made of stern stuff. Aditya slowly clawed his way back from immobility, refusing to give in to the continual and excruciating pain, or allowing what he now called the 'limping gait of the Maratha' to hinder his lifestyle in any way. With characteristic craftiness he had procured a half-price ticket for me to travel by train as a disabled person's attendant and we were now on our way from Delhi to Jabalpur in central India where we were to visit Tara.

'Do you really, truly think she'll recognise me?' I asked Aditya yet again.

'Oh Mighty Shiva, Lord of all the Universe, give me patience,' Aditya moaned, steepling his fingers together, as if in prayer, and closing his eyes wearily. 'How many times do I have to tell you, elephants never forget. You rescued her from a life of hell, lugged her halfway across India and found her a home where she lives in luxury. I mean, how on earth could she forget? Or anybody else involved for that matter,' he muttered underneath his breath. Then he added, 'and anyway, you've been back to see her since our journey four years ago. You told me she was always delighted to see you . . .'

'Yes, yes, I know all that,' I interrupted, 'but this is the longest time I've been without seeing her. More than eighteen months. Remember what Bhim said. See mummy by six months. Haathi do forget.'

'That was just emotion,' Aditya said dismissively. 'Or more likely rum. Bhim, bless the old rascal's socks, would say or do anything after a few shots. But I have a feeling, my friend' – his eyes began to glitter like those of a cat playing with a mouse – 'that's not the real reason for all this panic.'

I squirmed. 'I don't know what you're talking about.'

'Oh yes you do!' – the mouse now firmly between the cat's paws. 'You're worried about telling her, aren't you?'

He was right. To be honest, each time I had visited Tara in the past I had dreaded being greeted as a total stranger, but she had always received me with affection. This time was different. I was about to make another journey by elephant. Without Tara. I felt a cad and was convinced she would be upset by my treachery. No doubt, in the minds of most people, travelling several hundred miles across India simply to tell an elephant that you are deserting her would be considered at the least eccentric, and perhaps bordering on lunacy. I did not care, she deserved to know. After all, Tara was no ordinary elephant. She was a lady, and I liked to think I was a gentleman. It seemed to me the decent thing to do.

'I wouldn't be too worried about Tara,' Aditya added. 'She's a sweetheart – she'll forgive you. If I were you I'd be more worried about the new woman in your life.'

Aditya was referring to Parbati Barua, a mysterious figure whose name had cropped up constantly during our last journey with Tara. We had heard her discussed in hushed and reverent tones by the old mahouts at night around the campfires and at the elephant fair at Sonepur. Her father was the late Prince Prakitish Chandra Barua of Gauripur in Assam, more familiarly known as Laljee – a legend among that strange and secretive fraternity of elephant handlers; the greatest elephant expert in all Asia, he was believed to have an almost mystical affinity with elephants.

It was extraordinary that, out of his large family, he had chosen Parbati, a young daughter, to inherit his mantle. Shunning normal female conventions, Parbati had followed in his footsteps. Her entire life had been spent living and working with elephants in the remote jungles of Bengal and Assam in north-east India.

Parbati had been at the Sonepur Mela that very year when I had arrived with Tara. Desperate to find my beloved elephant a good home, I had searched for Parbati, but mysteriously she had disappeared. Every time Aditya and I returned on a nostalgic pilgrimage to Sonepur hoping to find Parbati Barua, we had heard she was there, and each time she had vanished. It was like chasing a myth.

The wheel, however slowly, had turned full circle. Now at last I was to meet her. She was to become my teacher, and together we would embark on another elephant journey.

3

'Why on earth should I be worried about *her*?' I asked Aditya in bewilderment. 'I'm sure she's charming. After all, her name – Parbati – means Mother Goddess. And what's more,' I continued, eager to impress the Maratha with my knowledge of the Hindu deities, 'Parbati is also the Mother of Ganesh, the elephant-headed God of protection. So what could be more appropriate. It'll be a piece of cake.'

'In her benevolent form, my friend, she's known as Parbati. But our deities,' he explained smugly, 'unlike your boring old God, can transform themselves. In her grim aspect she can become Kali, or even Chandi, who is often depicted as a horrible hag with fierce carnivore's tusks, a red tongue lolling from her mouth, and wearing a garland of skulls. It all depends on her mood.'

I swallowed hard. 'Well, I'm sure we'll get on splendidly.'

I

A Pampered Princess

L ike most great journeys, it is only on returning home that the full impact of the experience takes effect. Elephants, like India herself, move slowly and subtly to educate humans – and Tara had been a clever and seductive teacher. What had started as a whim soon turned into a passion for the Asian Elephant, and now it had become an obsession. With Tara I had learnt that these majestic and beautiful animals were teetering on the brink of extinction – and what was more, the conservation-conscious western world seemed indifferent to this impending tragedy.

Once Asian elephants roamed in their millions from Syria to China. Now they are reduced to pathetic little herds in equally reduced forest fragments. Today it is doubtful if as many as fifty thousand elephants survive in the wild in the whole of Asia, compared with Africa's growing population of over half a million.

Unlike the larger, mammoth-tusked African elephant, the Asian elephant does not suffer to the same extent from poaching because only certain males carry ivory. It is the loss of natural habitat on a vast scale, due to the massive increase in population, that is pushing the elephant towards extinction in Asia.

Ironically, the African elephant has benefited from a highly emotional public outrage at the bloody slaughter for ivory. Appeals to help fund its survival have been so lucrative, positive and widespread that the Asian elephant, like the proverbial poor relation, has remained in the background, waiting patiently for some crumbs. It seemed to me that the world had forgotten there was another elephant.

On returning to England after my expedition with Tara I became what is now socially fashionable in major western capitals – a person with a cause. But – to borrow an Indian expression – what to do? Not much, it seemed. I contacted countless elephant charities. How could I help? Efficient and enthusiastic young things would brightly extol the amazing progress that was being made. Donations were welcome by credit card, cheque, postal-order and even cash. Every penny counts, they would state earnestly. You could make a difference . . . If you want to make it more personal we have a new scheme: you can adopt a baby elephant that's lost its mother . . . Poaching has dropped by ninety per cent since the ivory ban . . . The African elephant is really making a dramatic . . .

Excuse me, I would interrupt politely. I want to help the other elephant – you know, the smaller and prettier one that lives, or is trying to live, in Asia.

Oh, would be the reply, is there a problem?

It was like beating your head against a wall. I even attended a Charity Gala Ball, supposedly to raise funds for all elephants. At fifty quid a pop, it was a glitzy and expensive affair, and as the evening wore on, it became more expensive – the climax being a Gala Auction.

The next morning I was awakened by one of the event's organisers. 'Thank you *so* much!' she trilled down the telephone, piercing my hangover. 'Your enthusiasm was absolutely tremendous!' She then listed the lots that I had bought at auction: a discotheque for the evening of my choice and a Zandra Rhodes frock.

For months I moped around disconsolately. In India I had bought a beautiful and extremely large wooden elephant mounted on wheels, perhaps the discarded plaything of some past Maharajah's favourite child. In my flat, surrounded by pictures of Tara, I rode this wooden pachyderm round and round the sitting-room, much to my wife's growing despair, like some mad urban mahout – all dressed up and nowhere to go.

Then one day the telephone rang and I found myself talking to an independent television producer who wanted me to make a second journey across India with Tara, for a documentary film. For a moment, my spirits soared, then just as rapidly, crashed. I hardly felt that an audience would be glued to their screens for two hours, watching an Englishman struggling across India on an elephant. Anyway, I had already done it once, and the magic would not be there a second time. Besides, how would this focus on the plight of the Asian elephant in the wild? The route he was suggesting was hardly elephant country.

More important, I was worried about Tara. At that particular moment, there was nothing I would have liked better than to set off with her again. She would, I knew, give me back my confidence, but she would have had to travel by truck to the location suggested by the film producer, and past experience told me how much she hated trucks. I knew I was making the right decision in refusing his offer. Tara now had a perfect life.

Then I remembered Parbati Barua. Here was the perfect solution. I told the producer about this extraordinary woman. She owned elephants; she was reputed to possess extraordinary knowledge and skills; she worked in an area of India, the northeast, where the Asian elephant was perhaps facing its toughest battle for survival; and, best of all she was a woman. It seemed to me an unbeatable combination. He agreed.

Once again, I called on the charity of my Indian friends. Miraculously, they tracked Parbati down. Even more miraculously, she agreed to the proposal. I then contacted Aditya. He accepted the challenge without hesitation. His chief role was to be the stills photographer, but in truth I would not have undertaken any journey in India without him. His friendship, his diplomatic skills and a lifetime's knowledge of all things Indian had been invaluable on the adventure with Tara. In the meantime, backing from one of America's most successful satellite channels was arranged. I had a chance to fulfil a dream. I was going to ride elephants with the legend herself. Little did I know what I was letting myself in for.

The train pulled into Jabalpur, a sleepy cantonment town situated almost in the centre of India. In 1911, when the British decided to move the capital of British India from Calcutta, only the toss of a coin settled that Delhi rather than Jabalpur would be Calcutta's successor. Still, snooker had been invented in the officers' mess at Jabalpur, and as we began the five-hour drive by car due east of the city to Tara's home at Kipling Camp, I noticed that some areas still retained signs of their colonial origins. Behind neatly-trimmed privet hedges crumbling porticoed bungalows, almost strangled by bougainvillaea, sat solidly and a little sadly like overgrown flowerpots at the end of spacious lawns.

In a local market, I bought my secret weapon – crisp, fresh and tangy *gur* (or unrefined sugar). If this didn't console Tara, nothing would.

'I see you're taking no chances,' Aditya remarked, reclining languidly on the back seat of the car as he watched me struggle to lift another 20-kilo sack into the dickie.

'It's just a little gift. Tara loves gur. I always bring her some.'

'Some little gift,' he muttered, as the car groaned and squeaked and subsided another few inches to the ground. 'Bribe, more likely.'

Aditya was right – the way to Tara's heart had always been in part through her stomach. But such was my anxiety that I was taking no chances. Then another thought struck me. Not only was I deserting her, I was also stopping her from becoming a film star – and Tara's vanity was not something to be taken lightly. Was I going completely mad? Mercifully, as soon as I climbed back into the car, I fell asleep.

When I awoke some hours later, a large full moon was painting the entire landscape silver. So bright was it that headlights were unnecessary. I roused Aditya.

'It's a full moon,' I shouted.

'I'm not blind,' he said.

'But remember all that old Indian hocus-pocus you used to bang on about – how events on the day of the full moon were always auspicious, always lucky. Think where we were exactly four years ago. At the Sonepur Mela. It was Kartik Purnima [the celebration of the full moon]. And it was that day we found Tara a new home. Now, here we are, under a full moon again, about to be reunited with her. I know everything's going to be all right – for Tara – for our new journey. It's fate. We're blessed.'

'Well, if I were you, my friend,' Aditya replied, 'I might take heed of a bit of old English hocus-pocus.'

'What d'you mean?'

'Oh, just that old English superstition,' he said innocently. 'Elephants, like women, never forget an injury.'

*

It was late when we reached Kipling Camp. I asked the driver to turn off the engine and headlights and we coasted silently down the soft, sandy track to Tara's residence. Illuminated in a shaft of moonlight, sprawled in comfort on a mountain of fodder, dwarfed by the ceilings of her immense home, lay Tara – a princess in her castle, snoring stentoriously. I tried to jump from the car, but Aditya stopped me.

'Let her sleep,' he whispered. 'You know she hates to be woken up. She'll probably have a heart attack if she sees us. We'll visit her in the morning.'

As if to agree with this decision, she rolled her fat bottom into a more comfortable position, stretched her legs, farted loudly and continued with her dreams.

That night I tossed and turned, unable to sleep, such was my anxiety and excitement. At five o'clock, I forced the grumbling Maratha out of bed. We walked down to the edge of the camp. The mist was still heavy on the ground, enveloping us in a filmy curtain. Gradually it lifted and I saw her. A lump rose in my throat.

She was standing in a pile of fodder, making short work of a tree trunk that was disappearing into her mouth like a carrot being pushed into a blender. I called her name. She pricked her ears in puzzlement and extended her trunk, testing the air. Then she let out that familiar sound – a kind of half-sneeze, half-squeak,

9

like a large deflating rubber ball. Excitedly, she waved her trunk up and down, as if beckoning me. I needed no encouragement. I rushed over, wrapped my arms around her trunk and planted a huge, smacking kiss on her eye. She curled her trunk around me, drawing me into her body and rumbled deeply in her throat. All the anxiety drained out of me. I realised that it would make no difference if it was eighteen months or eighteen years, she would always know me. I felt the familiar cold tip of her trunk exploring my body. I had secreted several lumps of gur in various pockets. These were rapidly discovered and even more rapidly disappeared into her soft pink mouth.

Aditya had kept his distance, respectful of my emotions. But he, too, could not contain himself any longer and limped towards her. He had not seen her for four years. Before he could greet her, she did something so uncanny it was hard to believe my eyes. She extended her trunk and gently explored the side of his arm where, four years before, at the Sonepur Mela, Aditya had suffered another bad accident and severely burnt himself.

'I told you so,' he said, although I could see that he was as shaken as I was by this extraordinary action. 'Elephants never forget an injury . . . but I must say', he continued, studying her carefully, 'she's certainly lost her figure.'

Unfortunate, but true. She was immense. Her belly almost touched the ground. This was all to be corrected by her new mahout, Singhal, a Rajput from Rajasthan, a lean and muscular man who was watching all this fuss with a certain amused detachment. Singhal had orders from my old friend, Bob Wright, who now cared for Tara, to put her on a strict diet and to improve her manners. Mujeem, her previous mahout, had almost killed her with kindness. A spoilt and petulant elephant can become a dangerous elephant. These are highly intelligent animals, and unless you impose some kind of discipline, they will exploit you mercilessly and sometimes fatally.

One incident had finally convinced Bob that Mujeem had to be replaced. Domesticated elephants become totally dependent on their mahouts. In fact, mahouts become an elephant's family, but an elephant wants a happy family and no animal is quicker to detect bad vibrations.

Tara's palatial home had been constructed in such a way that her mahout and her *chaarkatiya*, or food gatherer, lived in little rooms which opened up on to her courtyard. It was designed in this way for good reason because elephants hate to be lonely. The arrangement works well if the members of the elephant's family get on with each other. Unfortunately, Mujeem and the chaarkatiya did not. There were regular arguments, due perhaps to jealousies and, of course, to drink.

One morning, following a particularly bad argument with Mujeem, the chaarkatiya took Tara to collect her fodder. Still upset and probably suffering from a severe hangover, he vented his rage on Tara, slashing her trunk with his axe. The following day he was standing on her back cutting a high branch when she took a step sideways. He fell and broke his leg.

The incident finally convinced Bob that both Mujeem and the chaarkatiya had to go. I must say that I missed Mujeem. For all his faults, the old mahout genuinely adored Tara and, although he was entitled to three weeks' holiday each year, he had always returned after only five or six days away because he missed her. As I inspected Tara, I found that, like me, Mujeem had taken a memento – her tail feathers, the long, springy hair that decorates the tip of an elephant's tail, were decidedly more sparse.

Although most elephants live in fairly primitive and functional *pilkhanas*, or stables, this had not been the case with Tara. Over the years, Bob and I had become harassed and over-worked architects, trying to satisfy the whims of our spoiled client. Each time we had constructed what we thought would be suitable and comfortable, Tara had shown her displeasure by pulling the entire construction down. Eventually, fed up with these fits of pique, we had designed something on the scale of St Paul's Cathedral. Even if she were to stand on her back legs, which she could not do because she was too fat, that strong and powerful proboscis would wave impotently in the air, unable to reach the enticing beams that lay above her.

Everything in the pilkhana had been designed for her comfort. The solid brick walls which surrounded her on three sides were perforated by small openings, allowing cool air to pass through during the hot monsoon months. No expense had been spared when designing her bathroom. A polished stone floor had been carefully angled so that when she relieved herself – which was often – her urine would run directly into a neat little drain that ran along one side of the building. Her immense droppings were cleared almost before they had thudded to the floor, and, of course, her larder was constantly replenished with a mountain of fresh fodder.

Even interior decoration had been taken into consideration. Facing her hung a huge portrait taken by Aditya, showing her in a very flattering and beautiful pose, and on the surrounding walls were all her trappings, her *gudda* (saddle), her howdah and all her ropes and chains, neatly arranged.

It was an estate agent's dream. I could imagine the particulars – a large converted barn with unusually high ceilings, tastefully decorated in a rustic way, with excellent bathroom facilities, large kitchen (with live-in staff) and the added bonus of a small, but well-kept garden overlooking a magnificent vista. I would happily have moved in myself.

*

Anna Leonowens, a resident at the Court of Siam in the latter half of the nineteenth century described how a sacred and royal white elephant would be taken for his bath:

> When his lordship would refresh his portly person in the bath, an officer of high rank shelters his noble head with a great umbrella of crimson and gold, while others wave golden fans before him. On these occasions, he is invariably preceded by musicians who announce his approach with cheerful minstrelsy and songs

Without quite the pomp and circumstance, but certainly in my case with the same concern, Tara's portly person was made ready for me to ride her down to the river for her bath. And portly was the right word. As I settled on to her broad back, my legs were forced apart like a pair of rusty old calipers. She had not only expanded sideways, she seemed to have grown too – it looked a very long way down. But, with a sharp command of 'Agit' from me, she lumbered slowly forwards and then, as I dug my toes behind her ears, she gathered momentum and settled into that familiar rock n' roll rhythm.

From a riding point of view, Singhal had certainly whipped her into shape. In the old days she had meandered from side to side and stopped frequently to fill her stomach. Now riding her was like driving a Bentley – well, perhaps a vintage Bentley. She even took her snacks on the move, as overhanging branches were snapped off with a quick flick of her trunk.

Running my fingers affectionately through the carpet of vertical hair on her head, which gave her the appearance of a punk rocker, I shouted down to the limping Aditya, who was having trouble keeping up with us.

'How do I look?'

'You want an honest answer?' he said breathlessly, his face covered with sweat.

'Of course,'

'Fatter and older.'

We reached the river. Her bathing pool was deep and inviting, swollen by the monsoon rains. Beneath me, Tara began to vibrate violently, a sure sign of an elephant's unease. I knew better. In Tara's case it was excitement. All elephants love water. With Tara water was an obsession. Once she got in, you could not get her out again. Singhal had experienced this little quirk of hers a few days earlier. It had taken him eleven hours to entice her out of the water, and even then she only came because she was cold and bored. Secretly I loved this playful side of her. The last time I was here, I had joined her enthusiastically in the deep and wide pools, enjoying her aquatic acrobatics. Now I respected Singhal's position. A mahout's life was hard enough without having to waste all day pandering to the fantasy of an elephant that thought it was a dolphin. I quickly dismounted and, before she had a chance to blink, grabbed the chains and hobbled her two front feet together. I could hardly look her in the eye – I knew I had spoilt her fun as I led her, shuffling, like a prisoner into the pool. For two hours Singhal and I worked on her, scrubbing every inch of that huge body until she shone like obsidian.

To get back in favour after her bath, I surreptitiously fed her a packet of biscuits. This was a mistake, for it just whetted her insatiable appetite. Spying my T-shirt, she shot out her trunk and popped it into her mouth. Then, with an expression of pure bliss, she farted loudly and began to search around for more goodies.

Singhal reprimanded her, rapping her trunk with a small springy stick. He explained that she was attracted by the salt from the sweat in my T-shirt. Still, it was unforgivable, he told me, and it would not happen again. I suspected it had less to do with salt than greed. After all, elephants have been known to eat the strangest of things. I had read recently that Judy, an Asian elephant in an English zoo, had twice swallowed her keeper's radio, and on both occasions it had appeared the next day from Judy's other end, a little cleaner and in full working order. I did not hold out much hope for my T-shirt.

We rode slowly home. Aditya reclined beside me on the howdah.

'So,' he asked, 'when are you going to tell her? I wouldn't leave it too long, if I were you. We'll be leaving in a few days and she'll have to get used to the idea.'

'I'm not going to tell her.'

'What! After all you've put me through,' he retorted. His good humour disappeared. 'You're just a typical Englishman. No heart. I always tell my dog when I'm going away.'

'Really?' This was a side of the Maratha I did not know.

'Well, not quite to your extent,' he stuttered, embarrassed. 'But animals do have feelings. You know . . .'

'I'm well aware of that, but I think she'll tell me.'

He stared at me in pity. 'Now you've really gone bonkers.'

Maybe I had, but Tara was a very unusual elephant, and on our last journey she had been my teacher. She had always managed to communicate her knowledge in some little way. Once, when I had tried to force her too fast along a rocky road, she had picked up some stones in her trunk and placed them on her head to inform me that her feet were hurting. I was convinced that if I opened my mind she would give me a sign.

Over the next few days I took her for long rides into the thick forest where we collected her fodder. In the early evenings we took baths together. We invented some new games – including tug-of-war with my sarong. In another test of strength, I would push against her trunk with all my might. To start with she would let me win and retreat a few steps. Then, with a flick of her trunk she would send me sprawling away into the sand. Afterwards she would come trotting up, kick sand in my face like an overgrown bully, and demand another round.

Tara had always been fastidious. After her bath, she would pick up a little stick in her trunk and use it to clean between her toes. Now I was to be honoured with this task. She selected the stick, gave it to me and gently placed each of her massive front feet in turn in the palm of my hand. She would then stand with a blissful expression on her face while I carefully carried out my duties as her personal beautician.

As each idyllic day passed the bond between Tara and me grew stronger. It was as if we had never been apart. My happiness, however, was clouded by a sense of unease at my imminent departure, and I watched her behaviour for any change of emotion.

If her demonstrations of affection towards me were anything to go by, it seemed as if she would literally never want to let me go. Using her two small protruding tushes and her long narrow lip as a kind of vice, she would happily squeeze my head. I tended to forget that Tara was no ordinary pet. She was a large, adult elephant and, like all big and gentle creatures, whether human or animal, she sometimes forgot her own strength. Inevitably, the pain became so great that I had to punch her hard on her trunk to release me. She would then stand looking at me with a bemused expression on her face, as if to say: what on earth have I done wrong? To this day, I still bear the scars – two small indentations just above my ears, resulting from Tara's version of a goodnight kiss.

'I could retire here,' I said wistfully to Aditya as we huddled around the small fire in Tara's house, watching Singhal prepare her favourite appetiser – thick, doughy chapatties. Behind him, Tara waited, crouched and concentrated like a slip fielder. At intervals, Singhal would pick up a chapatti from the growing pile and flick it over his shoulder like a frisbee. Tara would deftly field it, wave it around in her trunk to allow it to cool, then pop it into her mouth. She would then assume her former pose and wait for the next delivery.

'I can just imagine it,' I continued, 'a sort of Indian Family Robinson – my children playing with Tara's children and . . .'

'You haven't got any children,' Aditya interrupted. He pointed at Tara. 'As for that spinster, she's far too old.'

Not even Aditya could be permitted to insult my elephant.

'Nonsense, Tara's only thirty-something. Just the other day in England a sixty-two-year-old elephant gave birth. . .'

'Okay, Okay,' he said. 'But, we have to get going. We've been here far too long already. You have a date with another lady, and I wouldn't keep *her* waiting.'

'You're right,' I said, 'I'll tell Tara tonight.'

As it turned out, it was not necessary. Tara, as I always believed she would, told me.

To commemorate our last evening together, Aditya, Singhal and I decided to have a few drinks. As I opened the bottles of rum, I noticed Tara looking longingly at the liquor. How thoughtless of me not to include her – Tara always enjoyed a drop or two. Grabbing a torch, I went into the little store at the back of her stable to fetch her wine glass – a large bucket.

It was dark in the storeroom. As I searched for the bucket the weak beam of the torch illuminated a dull reddish cloth poking out from under a pile of old sacking. Somehow it looked familiar. I pulled back the sacking and discovered the old red cushion that had protected my backside from the hard surface of the howdah on which Tara had carried me eight hundred miles across India. Underneath the cushion, I discovered another old friend – Tara's saddle. The memories came flooding back of those evenings spent around the campfire and of Bhim, a cigarette clamped between two yellow stumps of teeth, painstakingly patching up and repairing this most important item of an elephant's pack gear with a rusty needle. Now it lay discarded, forgotten, its stuffing exploding from its guts like an old and unloved teddy bear.

Overcome by nostalgia, I dragged it out into Tara's stable to show Aditya. I had hardly got through the door when a large branch crashed into the wall beside me. I took cover – only just in time. Like an artillery officer, she had found her range. Emitting a shrill trumpet, she lobbed another missile over her shoulder which struck the ground just in front of the saddle.

For one self-deluded moment I mistook this fit of rage for a sign of excitement. Then Singhal rushed towards me, weaving and ducking through the increasing barrage of hurled objects, grabbed the saddle and quickly threw it back into the store-room. Tara had become a pampered odalisque. There was no way that she was going to put on her rucksack and hit that road again.

With the saddle hidden, peace in the pilkhana was restored and glasses were refilled. As I watched Tara sip happily and noisily from her wine glass, I knew with absolute certainty that no other elephant could ever take her place in my heart. But I did not feel sad – I was elated. The remainder of our lives would be inextricably linked, and whenever I needed reassurance she would always be here; huge, happy and understanding.

The next morning I shouted goodbye as we drove past her palace. She simply raised her trunk and then continued with her breakfast. The car turned the corner, and I could have sworn I heard a sigh of relief.

2

In at the Deep End

Two days later, Aditya, the television film producer and I were on our way to Bagdogra, a busy air force base strategically positioned in that strange little corner of North India that is bordered by Nepal in the west, Sikkim and Bhutan to the north, Bangladesh to the south and, just over the mighty Himalayas, the vast and brooding menace of China. Bagdogra was once a small village renowned for its abundance of tigers. In Bengali it means 'the place of the roaring tigers'. Nowadays the roar is of a different kind as thousands of pounds of aviation fuel propel the MiG jets of the Indian air force hourly into the air to patrol the borders of this sensitive and isolated outpost.

From Bagdogra, we headed by jeep towards the town of Siliguri, where we were to meet the legendary Parbati Barua herself. As we drove, the whole panorama of the Himalayas unfolded before us. From the yellow mass of pollution that hung like a dirty carpet over Siliguri, precipitous hills climbed in jostled masses and long ridges to form the backbone of this mighty and most noble of all mountain ranges. A few of the peaks were already dappled with snow; further to the north towered Kanchenjunga – a magic white citadel, sharp as a diamond in that rarefied air.

We descended into the chaos of Siliguri – a sprawling industrial town and the main terminus for thousands of trucks heading north to Nepal and Bhutan and east to Assam. 'Siliguri', I had discovered, meant 'stony site' in the native patois of the area, for it was the furthest point at which the boulders from the Himalayas still appeared on the surface of the muddy Delta of Bengal. Unfortunately those boulders have long been crushed and probably used to forge the bland and uninspired mish-mash of Indian architecture which is so prevalent among the growing metropolises of the subcontinent. No better example of this architectural awfulness existed than our destination. Sinclair's Hotel looked exactly like a long, thin, cement prison block built on three floors. But it boasted an aqua club which, the manager informed me, was most refreshing. I tentatively dipped a toe in the pool. It did not tempt me. The water was dark green and icy and, apart from a lone frog doing lengths, deserted.

I was now beginning to feel uneasy. Soon I was to meet the person who had floated ethereally in and out of my elephant life for the last four years, someone who, if she wanted, could teach me more about these magnificent animals than I could ever hope to learn otherwise. I was not just here to make a film. For me Parbati Barua represented the ultimate guru, and, as I knew from past experience, first impressions are so important.

I had argued relentlessly with the film producer about this first encounter. I had insisted that I spend a few days getting to know her by myself. What would happen if she didn't like me? After all, I was a complete stranger, a male and a foreigner, and she was an Indian woman. Indian etiquette is very strict. That was something I had already learnt.

The producer was adamant. He wanted spontaneity and proceeded to baffle me with such Hollywood jargon as 'bonding and interaction' and likened our meeting to Tom Cruise, as a young pilot in the film *Top Gun*, being thrown into the proverbial deep end. At that moment I felt like throwing him into the deep end of the aqua club pool.

Yet who was I to argue with the demands of the celluloid world? I knew nothing about film-making. I was just a student who had come to learn about elephants from one of Asia's great masters. It was into this minefield of awkwardness that I stepped to meet Parbati Barua as I entered the faded velour dining-room of Sinclair's Hotel.

*

If it had not been for the presence of the producer, Aditya and the District Forest Officer, I would have thought I was in the wrong place. Dwarfed by the three men was a tiny young woman dressed in a simple cotton beige and crimson sari, a cosy plum-coloured cardigan with pearl buttons draped across her narrow shoulders. She was clutching a large, navy-blue leather handbag. This petite figure, still in her thirties, looked more like an Indian Mrs Tiggywinkle than one of India's greatest elephant experts.

I found myself staring in astonishment. Was this a joke? Could this little waif of a woman, whose waist was slimmer than one of my thighs and whose delicate wrists were encircled by simple gold bracelets, possibly be the legendary character I had heard discussed in reverent tones by the mahouts around the campfires at Sonepur? Was she the one who, as a teenager, had lassoed and caught her own elephant?

Pulling myself together, I steepled my hands, greeting her in the traditional Indian manner. It was only when she acknowledged my greeting and lifted her head that I began to think a little differently. It was her eyes. I had never seen anything like them. They were black – but hell black – and bored into one's skull with the intensity of a laser. They demanded obedience. I wondered what effect they had on an elephant, as I found myself transfixed like a rabbit in front of a cobra.

I do not remember sitting down, only finding myself squeezed into a chair next to her, my legs awkwardly protruding from shorts in front of me. I felt huge and clumsy, horribly aware of my pink thighs, set like jelly in a mould in the confines of the chair. Too late, I knew I should have worn long trousers.

For once, I was at a loss for words. The producer was discussing the proposed route and the film with the District Forest Officer, whose assistance and local expertise was to prove invaluable. Aditya, with all the charm and courtesy of a man born into Indian nobility, was chatting easily with Parbati. This respite, at least, gave me the chance to study her.

A mass of thick black hair, neatly parted and pulled tightly back in one long knotted tress, almost touched the floor. Her proud and handsome face was accentuated by high cheekbones and thick eyebrows that seemed to have a life of their own as they danced like bat wings up and down her forehead. She smiled suddenly at something that Aditya said. The top of her lip curled upwards exposing perfectly white, even teeth except for one sharp little fang that gave her an almost feral look, like a tiny exquisite wild animal. And like all wild animals, she possessed the ability to remain absolutely still. When she moved it was like the flutter of a hummingbird's wing – quick, controlled and economical – and I sensed a steely strength within.

Aditya had noticed my discomfort. He suggested that I show Parbati my book. It was a brilliant solution to my paralysis. She flipped quickly through the pages and stopped at a photograph of Tara. I sensed a softening in this diamond bright creature.

'Beautiful elephant,' she murmured, 'about forty, maybe more.'

'How do you know?' I instantly regretted speaking. She looked up and locked in those lasers.

'I know!' she snapped.

I sank further into my chair. She turned to the end of the book. One of the last photographs portrayed me using Tara as a cushion while writing at Kipling Camp. The lasers locked in again, this time with even greater intensity.

'What you do here?' she demanded.

'Well,' I stammered, 'it was the end of the journey. I had become very close to Tara and I was, well, you know . . .'

'It is not just enough to love elephants,' she interrupted. 'You do not know how quickly they can turn. Never show your back to elephant.'

I hung my head in shame. Sensing my embarrassment she patted me on the arm. 'I know what you are feeling. I make many mistakes when I was a child. My papa chided me also. Do not worry. You will learn.' With that she turned to Aditya.

I felt like a schoolboy. Again I cursed the producer for this insensitivity. This was not a good beginning. Filming started tomorrow. The crew were due to arrive that night and we would meet Parbati and her elephants at a camp she had established at a place called Murti, some forty miles north-east of Siliguri. As we said our farewells Parbati told us not to be late.

'6 a.m. Greenwich time, not IST. I do not work on Indian Standard Time. Elephants cannot be kept waiting.'

She swept out imperiously.

'Well,' the producer said, 'I think that went jolly well, don't you?'

I muttered under my breath and went to find Aditya. He was standing by the pool studying the frog which was still ploughing up and down.

'Listen,' I hissed, 'that was a disaster.'

'Don't worry my friend. Everything is under control. We are going to see Parbati later. Alone. Tonight. Before work starts in the morning.'

'How on earth did you manage that?' I asked, relief flooding over me.

'It had nothing to do with me. It was her. She wants to meet with you. She feels just as uneasy as you do.'

'One thing's for sure,' I said soberly, 'this isn't going to be the happy ramble across India we had with Tara. It will be like going back to school. What have I let myself in for – again?'

'Welcome to my country again, Mr Shand,' Aditya said in a thick Indian accent. 'I will be showing you many wondrous tings. Meanwhile let us be getting liquor. We will be shoving off at four o'clock.'

★

Chauffeured by one of the many drivers hired for this epic, a timid Buddhist called Soni, we drove out of Siliguri suitably fortified for our meeting with Parbati.

We crossed a high graceful bridge spanning the cold rushing waters of the Teesta river, which rises high in Lake Chalamó in Tibet and, curiously, means quiet. An unsuitable name, I thought, for the icy torrent that raged hundreds of feet below.

'Beautiful bridge,' I remarked to Aditya, 'British, of course?'

'Coronation Bridge,' he replied in a matter-of-fact tone. 'Total length of 563 feet with a span of 260 feet and a rise of 132 feet. The piers and the arches are all hollow, and this was the first bridge of such magnitude in India in which hollow box construction was adopted. The bridge was designed by Mr John Chambers and was opened by His Excellency Sir John A. Herbert, Governor of Bengal, on the 12th of March 1941.'

I stared at him in astonishment. 'How on earth do you know that?'

'I studied British architecture at university,' he replied, 'amongst other things, of course – lepidoptery, ornithology, economics, classical English and history. It's a pity you were such a dunce at school. It is essential, I find, to have a good education in this kind of work.'

I gave him a suspicious look. 'And I suppose you know all about the legend of the Teesta river?'

'What, that old rubbish about two rivers joining together? And how the male river gets pissed off with the female river because the female river has a straighter run. Even children know that. It's our equivalent of Humpty Dumpty.'

'Tell me then.'

'Well, if you insist. It goes something like this,' he began. 'In the beginning of the world . . .'

'Chuck the book over, Aditya.'

'What book?'

'The book you are reading from.'

Grinning, he handed me a massive tome. 'I thought it was a good thing to be prepared. A little light reading for those long nights at the camp. You know what the old Duke of Marlborough said, "Time in . . ." '

'Yes, yes,' I interrupted, 'time in reconnaissance is seldom wasted. Actually it was the Duke of Wellington.'

As we headed further east I began to wonder how elephants could possibly survive here. Apart from a thin ribbon of green which ran parallel to the foothills of the Himalayas, the forest was non-existent. Instead it was replaced by mile upon mile of tea gardens, interspersed by sprawling villages.

We stopped off at a hotel for a sharpener in a local town. Lying outside, a madman was lecturing his toes. Above him a sign announced, 'Cold Beer, Sold Here. Beer Cold, Here Sold'. The sign was no exaggeration. The beer was indeed ice cold.

At Gau-Dhuli, the hour of the cattle dust, when the setting sun turns everything golden, we turned into the tea estate where Parbati was based. For the last few years she, her mahouts and her elephants had been contracted by the tea estate management to drive out the wild elephants that maraud and damage the tea crops at night. She was also responsible for patrolling the irrigation ditches to flush out leopards. The females often delivered in these deep dark places because of the coolness and shade. Just a few days before one had attacked and killed a tea plucker.

We drove up to her little wooden house. She was waiting for us on the veranda, wearing a simple lungi and a yellow T-shirt which advertised a hotel in Hawaii. She was impatiently tapping her foot.

'Come up,' she said, 'and remove your shoes.'

Parbati's room was bare except for a small table and three wooden chairs. On the wall hung a little plaque, the only adornment in the room. It read:

> Where there is truth, there is religion.
> Where there is religion, there is prosperity.
> Where there is duty, there is nobility.
> Where there are elephants, there is victory.

It was written by a sage named Palakapya, who lived in Assam in the fifth or sixth century BC and is regarded as the founder of elephant lore, or *gaja-shastra*. Legend has it that he was born from an elephant and spent his life wandering with the wild herds, eating only the food they ate. He learnt all about their ailments and is reputed to be the author of a treatise on elephant medicine.

'Sit,' she said, as though commanding an elephant.

We sat. There was no lighting in the room except for a

24

small flickering candle. 'Who has been drinking?' she suddenly demanded. Aditya and I looked at one another.

'Er, well' – Aditya cleared his throat – 'we stopped on the way. We were hot and thirsty and . . .'

'Have you got drink?' she demanded again.

'Well, yes, in the car.'

'Go and get. I do not drink. But this is special occasion. We will drink to us.'

I grabbed a couple of bottles of beer from the car. Parbati produced three glasses and we clinked them together.

'*Jai Mata*, Victory to Goddess,' she toasted, and in one swallow she emptied the contents of a glass.

Aditya and I sneaked another look at each other. Things were improving. Parbati noticed our glance and smiled that strange, feral smile. Then she burst into laughter – a wonderful, earthy chuckle. It was so infectious we couldn't help joining in. Soon we were rocking backwards and forwards, tears running down our faces. The ice had been broken. I felt enormous relief.

It did not last long. Suddenly she switched back to her former imperious self. The change was so startling that I thought I was dealing with two completely different people. I wondered what her star-sign was. I made a bet with myself that she was a Gemini.

'Now, Mark, listen to me.'

I was all ears. I could hardly be otherwise.

'Many, many people have come to me to learn about elephants. I do not teach them. They are without heart. I think you have heart. I have heard about your journey with Tara. I think to myself, why this idiot want to ride elephant across India? Just a game, I thought. But then I hear you care for her. I can see it in your eyes. You love elephants, but too much. You must learn. Together we will do film. But it will be difficult. Too many people. But this film needs to be. People in world need to know how elephants are dying and how people are dying because they have taken elephants' land. But film and us different. We live in camp with my mahouts and sweeties. Film crew will be separate camp. We try not to think of film. We think of elephants, then we do good job. It is important always to do good job. Otherwise we both waste time.'

I interrupted her and asked what my duties as a mahout would be.

'Mahout!' she exclaimed. 'You are not mahout. Not until you prove yourself. You start at bottom, chaarkatiya – like me with my papa. I was born in my father's elephant camp. The first thing I saw when my eyes opened was elephant. Before ABC I learned elephant, jungle and shooting. One time when I was six, I was standing on the back of Papa's elephant. I fell off into thorn bush. Mahouts told Papa what happened. My papa said, Leave her, she has to learn. If she cannot stand on elephant, what good is she for me? So, same will be for you. You will listen and learn. You will be sore. You will be angry. I will be angry. I will tell you to be quiet. All these things I will do.'

Nervous, I lit a cigarette.

'And no smoking while riding elephants. How can you smell jungle? How can you tell danger when air is full of smoke?'

I glanced at Aditya. He was enjoying this.

'We will begin training', she continued, 'at elephant camp. When I think you are ready we will begin journey. Now,' she added kindly, 'go back, get sleep. You will need it. Tomorrow I introduce you to my elephants. You will love them. Like you love Tara.'

Oh my God, I thought to myself as I climbed wearily into the car, what on earth have I agreed to? But at least now everything was clear. For the next few months I would be a pupil and she my teacher. I could not complain. After all, it was what I had always wanted.

I had seldom seen Aditya so happy as we motored through the darkness. 'You, my friend, have had it. I am really going to enjoy this. For once I am going to sit back and relax. On our last journey I endured four months of you ordering me around. Now the boot is on the other foot. You're finished.' With a deep chuckle, he flicked the lid off another bottle of beer.

'Remember, Aditya, I'm going to be writing a book about this. Think of what I could write about you. You had better behave yourself as well. I'll be watching.'

'You wouldn't write badly about *me*, would you?'

'Trust me,' I said.

'You sound', he replied, 'exactly like Kaa the snake.'

The headlights of the jeep fleetingly illuminated the velvet coat of a pure black leopard as it glided like silk across the road.

'Stop the car!' Aditya yelled and started fumbling with the flash on his camera.

Instead Soni floored the accelerator, yelling 'Vood, vood.' Aditya was outraged and tried to grab the wheel. With the strength that comes from pure panic, Soni wrestled it out of Aditya's hands and we weaved and jerked down the road. Aditya questioned him angrily but he just kept repeating 'Vood, vood.'

'I can't understand him,' said Aditya with increasing annoyance. 'He's speaking in some weird dialect.'

'Vood, vood!' Soni shouted again.

Aditya started to laugh. 'You know what he's saying, Mark? Not "vood" but "hood". The poor bugger was terrified the leopard would leap on the roof and rip open the canvas top and kill us. Typical Buddhist.'

We named Soni 'Tiger' after that, for his bravery.

'Time for a nightcap,' Aditya said as we arrived back at the hotel. The bar was empty except for an old man with one arm, dressed in khaki mufti and nursing a glass of whisky.

'Planter,' Aditya whispered to me, 'I bet he's got some stories. Probably had his arm ripped off by a tiger. You sit down and relax. I'll go and rap with him.'

I had hardly sat down before Aditya returned.

'Well, any stories?' I asked.

'Er, no. The fellow's a German tourist.'

3
A Strange and Magical Woman

Early the next morning, in a clearing close to the banks of the river Murti and under the omnipresent eye of the camera which was to become part of our lives for the next few months, Parbati introduced me to her two elephants and her two mahouts, Phandika and Dino.

All four stared at me with the greatest suspicion – particularly the old man, Phandika. Even to my inexperienced eye I could see these nut-brown, tough, bow-legged men dressed in ill-fitting lungis and torn shirts were true professionals. I suddenly had a flashback to my old mahout, Bhim, when I first met him at the zoo in Bhubaneshwar – drunk and out of shape – a victim of the relatively easy life of the government servant compared to the independence and pride that I saw burn fiercely in the men who stood in front of me. I was going to have my work cut out. Not only would I have to try and break down the cultural barriers which separated us, I was going to have to prove myself to them, as well as to Parbati. I shook hands with Phandika. He growled something to Parbati, his voice hoarse from fifty years of shouting commands at elephants.

Nervously I asked, 'What did he say?'

She tried to keep a straight face. 'He ask, if you are elephant man, why your hands are soft.'

She beckoned to the eight tons of muscle that towered above her. Obediently the beasts shuffled over to her.

'Now Mark, come and meet my sweeties. Big one here is Lakhi Mala. She is garland of Goddess of Wealth. We call her Lakhi. And little one is Kanchen Mala. She is garland of gold. We call her Kanchen.' Both elephants simultaneously raised their trunks to me. 'See,' she said proudly, 'my sweeties are welcoming you. They are lovely, yes?'

Not half as lovely as Tara, I thought to myself. In fact, I was rather disappointed. I had expected one of Asia's greatest elephant experts to have great elephants. To my eyes, both her sweeties were rather lean and, compared to the polished gem of Tara, rather dirty. Lakhi was undoubtedly pretty, with beautiful long legs and a fine big head, but Kanchen – oh dear – she sagged everywhere and, worst of all, had pale eyes – a sure sign of a bad elephant, according to the Sanskrit texts.

I made my *namaste* to each of them and then reached out tentatively to pat them on their long thick trunks. Parbati, with uncanny intuition, a trait more common in wild animals, at once sensed my feelings.

'You do not like my elephants?' she said.

'Of course I do, Parbati, I love all elephants. It's just that I noticed Kanchen's eyes are pale. Isn't that a bad sign?'

I regretted my words the moment I had said them.

'Pah!' she exploded angrily and spat out of the corner of her mouth. 'Old bloody books. Old bloody humbugs writing books. It is not from books that you learn about these animals. It is from here' – she struck her forehead and then slapped the left side of her chest – 'and from here . . .'

'Oh no, Parbati, I just . . .'

'I know what you think,' she interrupted, 'I see in your eyes. You think of Tara. I understand that. Tara is your elephant, you love her. But Tara is not working elephant. My elephants work hard. My elephants are strong. My elephants are healthy and my elephants are busy. If elephant is not busy it is dangerous. They are cleverer than us. You must understand this. Already I see in photographs that Tara is too fat. I am thinking that soon Tara will do mischief. And after mischief sometimes comes death. Many mahouts I have seen killed by elephants.'

I listened in amazement and thought of Tara's problems with Mujeem and the chaarkatiya.

'Next time you see Tara, check mahout. Condition of elephants can be told from mahout. If mahout fat, mahout is lazy. Then elephant will be dangerous. Mark my words, I speak only truth. Look at my mahouts. They are strong. I trust them with my elephants. I am hard on them, but they respect me.'

It was then that I realised just how difficult it must have been for Parbati. She was a woman brought up in a totally male-dominated society, and she had overcome this barrier through sheer expertise and strength of character. She commanded, and demanded, the respect of all about her. Again I managed to put my foot in it. Anxious to get back in her good books, I told Parbati how beautiful I thought Lakhi was.

'She's much bigger than Tara,' I remarked. 'I haven't ridden an elephant for any distance for a long time. I'll be a little nervous on her.'

'On her!' Parbati snapped in derision, those bat wings of eyebrows bunched just above her eyes, 'Lakhi is my elephant. I caught her. I trained her. You are not fit for her. You will ride Kanchen. She is steady elephant. You will need steady elephant.'

The romantic image of myself astride a huge and magnificent elephant, gracing the screens of millions of households, disintegrated fast. Instead I would be more like a servant, legs akimbo on his donkey, struggling to keep up with the queen on her charger.

Still, I thought, as I imagined the bullying and the inevitable humiliation I was going to receive at the hands of this tigress over the next few months, I would not be the only one. The male sex was on the decline – women were taking over the world. It would be good training for the future.

I was at least relieved to have got something right – my clothes. Even that had not been easy. I had been up half the night trying to decide what to wear, like Ivana Trump before a ball. Not that I had much choice, especially as regards colour. Eventually I settled on green – a pair of old army fatigues and a matching T-shirt. I thought I would blend in rather well.

'First class,' Parbati said, eyeing me up and down with a nod of approval.

I returned the compliment. But she was in a different league. Mahatma Gandhi is said to have described the women of Assam as lovely. I agreed. She stood like a jewel draped in the traditional dress of a high-born Assamese woman – a beige mekla, of pure silk, the purple border delicately embroidered with a pattern of tiny running elephants.

'Just for camera,' she whispered conspiratorially out of the corner of her mouth, raising her eyebrows in resignation.

All the same, I sensed that she was delighted by my compliment. At that moment the facade had slipped a little, revealing another Parbati – a normal young woman, a little insecure, a little vulnerable, and genuinely flattered.

It did not last long. With a fluid movement she stooped to pick up a stone and flung it at a dog which was nosing around the cooking pots in the mahouts' camp, striking it hard on its backside. It yelped and shot off, squealing. She then yelled something quite unintelligible, which I could only imagine was a reprimand, to the two young boys who were hanging around the camp.

'They're my chaarkatiyas – beginners – like you . . . Now go and set up your tents. I will be back later.' In a shimmer of silk she disappeared.

'Well, my friend,' Aditya remarked as we stood in the elephant camp watching Phandika and Dino ride Lakhi and Kanchen into the forest to collect their fodder, 'what's it like to be a film star? Personally, after watching your debut performance, I don't think you quite possess the qualities of the great classical actors such as Olivier and Burton. Let me see. It's hard to place you . . .' His face screwed up in concentration. 'I have it,' he announced happily, 'you get everything wrong all the time. You're the fat one of Laurel and Hardy.'

I could see I was in for a long session on the movies and cut him off, leading him towards our old tents which we had used on the journey with Tara four years ago.

'Help me get our tents up. She'll be back soon.'

'*Our* tents? You mean yours and Parbati's tents. I've very comfortable accommodation over there.' Aditya pointed to the film crew's side of the river where a colourful army of triangles dotted a meadow like a Butlin's holiday camp. 'You should see it. Each tent has a lovely foam mattress. There is even a dining tent with china, knives and forks, chairs and a table, and there are dozens of people to cook and look after us. You see that?' He pointed to a larger, bright green canvas construction that resembled a Mogul emperor's hunting abode. 'That's the producer's tent. He's even got two proper beds in it. Anyway I intend to enjoy myself on this journey – in comfort and away from you.'

'You can't leave me to the mercy of Parbati,' I pleaded.

'Film stars on location always have their own private accommodation, and that's final. But I will help you put up your tents.'

'Okay then. You unfold them.'

Leaving Aditya to untangle the muddle of knots that bound up the tents, I wandered over to check out the mahouts' tiny shelter in which four men would sleep. It was a masterpiece of simplicity. A single sheet of canvas was slung over a framework of three bamboo poles, pulled tight and fixed to the ground with crude handmade wooden pegs. It was open on both sides, the back facing on to the elephants' pilkhana, a rectangular area shadowed by a large mango tree which had been cleared immaculately. A flattened pallet of straw served as bedding and small bundles containing their simple needs were wrapped in sarongs and acted as pillows. I winced as I thought of my brand new blue and red lilo, my crisp new sheets, my soft down sleeping-bag and the nice British Airways pillow that I had stolen on the flight.

Wedged under the side of the shelter were buckets, water containers and a selection of battered cooking utensils – a few big serving ladles, a couple of chopping knives and a few heavy pots and pans, all of which, I noticed, were spotlessly clean. On the other side, coiled neatly in rows, were the familiar trappings of elephant camps – thick manilla ropes and hand-forged chains.

At the back, the two young chaarkatiyas, Poni and Babul, were squatting over an ingenious stove, constructed from three smooth, oblong stones wedged vertically into the ground to form a circle.

They were stirring the contents of a steaming pot. They looked up, smiled shyly and then continued with their culinary duties. I hope she won't expect me to help, I thought to myself, as I watched them add pinches of salt and chilli. I loathed cooking.

There was even a small farmyard. The two heavy elephant saddles were propped against each other and in their shadow, a clutch of chickens, tied by their ankles to small sticks, were clucking happily as they pecked at the husks of rice which had been thrown down for them. On my way back to join Aditya, I stubbed my toe on something hard sticking out of the corner of the mahouts' tent. It was a half empty bottle of rum. Things were looking up.

By this time the presence of foreigners had drawn the inevitable crowd. I was relieved to see that most of them were hanging around gaping at the marvels of the holiday camp. A few had drifted over and were beginning to titter shyly as Aditya and I wrestled with our canvas monsters.

Holding the corners of our old tent, we flung it into the air to spread it out. As it billowed outwards, a cloud of fine dust hovered in the hot air. Instantly we were transported back four years to those long hot days on the road with Tara, to those campfires at the Mela, the air heavy with the scent of burning dung and the gentle chink of chains as six hundred tons of elephants settled down for the night around us. We smiled at one another – there was no need for words – both of us were locked in private recollections.

Memories of a different kind enveloped us as we spread out the smaller one – Bhim's tent. A blast of stale, fermented liquor, tobacco and urine nearly knocked us off our feet. As we shook it, a crumpled pack of bidis, a box of matches and a small medicine bottle, half filled with a clear liquid, fell out. I removed the cap.

'Yuk!' I said, wrinkling my nose and passing the bottle to Aditya. 'Smell that.'

'Mela Moonshine,' he declared, his nose twitching like a wine connoisseur, '1988 vintage. A slightly fruity bouquet. But it's aged well.' He tipped it down his throat. 'Delicious,' he said, his eyes watering.

'I can't let Parbati sleep in this. It's disgusting,' I said. 'I shall have to wash it.'

Aditya was outraged. 'You are supposed to be an English gentleman. Give Parbati our old tent; she's a woman. Have some bloody manners.'

'Well, Bhim's tent is smaller and she is small,' I argued weakly.

'She's the boss, my friend. Bosses always get the biggest – and you haven't exactly impressed her so far. This is your chance to curry some favour.'

Two hours later, sweating and exhausted, we sat back and admired our handiwork. We had done rather well. We had erected Parbati's tent close to the mahouts' and mine some distance away with the opening facing the mountains. This would give us both some privacy. I was a little apprehensive, to say the least, and quite naturally shy, about sleeping in such close proximity to a relative stranger – and a woman to boot.

Our satisfaction was cut short by the arrival of a self-important forest official. He informed us that we had pitched the tent on the path which the wild elephants use at night on their way to raid the surrounding paddy fields. We both laughed and ignored him. But he was most insistent, pointing to the rickety fence consisting of two strands of wire connected to tall poles that ran in an erratic line towards the hills.

'Electric fence,' he announced proudly, 'keep out haathi.'

We examined this construction with interest.

'Very effective, sir. Haathi touch, haathi explode.'

Aditya pointed out that our tents were on this side of the electric fence. For a moment the forest official looked perplexed. Then he beamed happily.

'Power cuts, sir. Many power cuts. Just last week haathi come through. Two house broken, one people broken.'

Noticing my packet of cigarettes, he helped himself to a handful and pushed off. Reluctantly we took down the tent and moved it closer to the elephant camp.

'Bloody Bengali windbag,' Aditya groaned, rubbing his bad leg. Wincing in pain, he lowered himself to the ground, stretched out and closed his eyes.

'Do you think that elephants really come through here?' I asked nervously.

'No chance,' Aditya murmured, 'he just wanted some of your fags.'

Within minutes he was fast asleep. I soon joined him.

*

I was awoken by a sharp, insistent banging on the back of my neck. Startled, I shot to my feet. Parbati stood behind me carrying two immense grey suitcases which she swung impatiently backwards and forwards with the utmost ease.

'Tent is in wrong place,' she announced. '*My* tent also in wrong place. Come.'

So much for my chivalry and good manners. I glared angrily at Aditya and pulled down my tent for the second time and carried it over to join Parbati. With the precision of an architect, she was slowly pacing out a small rectangular area, carefully marking it with small wooden sticks. She shouted something to Poni and Babul who came running over and were soon levelling the ground and removing stones.

'Tents will face inwards. My tent will go here. Fire will go there,' she said, pointing to a small area in the middle of the rectangle. 'Your tent will go here, opposite.'

I followed her directions with horror. By my calculations the distance between us would be no more than ten feet – I would look directly into her tent and vice versa. My privacy was now protected only by the fire. I made a mental note to build a bonfire on the scale of Guy Fawkes every night.

'Aditya's tent will go . . .' she continued – and then stopped. 'Where is Aditya's tent?'

The intense look of pleasure that had been spreading across his face disappeared.

'Er, Parbati, I'm camping over there with the crew. I'm not appearing in the film you see.'

'You are not camping with film crew,' she replied emphatically. 'You will stay with us. You are part of elephant camp. That is final.'

I could see Aditya's mind racing.

'I don't have a tent,' he argued weakly, 'and the crew tents are too conspicuous. In any case, it would have to be taken up and down during the filming and my leg is becoming too painful for all that. I get very tired nowadays.'

I said innocently, 'But I have a spare tent.' Aditya shot me a look of pure malice. 'It's one of those new domed climbing tents. Once it's up, you don't have to dismantle it. Just take out the pegs and move it. It's as light as a feather.'

I quickly assembled this strange bright purple bubble and carried it ceremoniously to its allotted position, equi-distant between Parbati and me.

'It looks like a frog,' Aditya said disdainfully. But all Indians love bright and new things, and Aditya, when he climbed inside, was quickly seduced by its charms. Soon he was filling the multitude of zippered pockets and pouches with film, cameras, books and booze.

After several more hours' work, the camp was erected to Parbati's satisfaction.

'See,' she said, clapping her hands together with glee, 'it is now like my papa's camps. Everything in order.' Clutching a small cluster of incense sticks, she made a quick *puja* in front of each tent to bless and protect our new home.

Later Aditya and I bathed in the crystal clear and icy waters of the Murti. Above us, rhesus macaque monkeys gambolled and chattered noisily in the overhanging branches. On the smooth boulders, bordering the edge of the torrent, groups of pied flycatchers sat motionless, like little chessboard pieces – only the constant flick of their tails disclosing their camouflage. And, to our left, perched on a branch of a petrified tree, a crested serpent-eagle glared at us, its yellow eyes furious that we had disturbed its vigil.

By the time Aditya and I got back from the river, Phandika and Dino had returned with the elephants and were untying the ropes that secured the fodder on their backs. Parbati appeared from nowhere and squatted down silently beside me on the bank. She nodded in approval as both elephants, on a command from

Phandika, simultaneously bent their back left legs and half a ton of deforestation crashed to the ground.

I watched Kanchen. Blinded by my absolute love for Tara, I realised that my first impressions of Kanchen might have been unfair. I could see – with a certain amount of relief – an innate kindness in her. Safety, I realised, not vanity, was the key to riding elephants and I now looked forward to our new relationship. As if Kanchen had read my mind, she stared at me intently, those beautiful, strange, pale eyes softening. Her look seemed to say, don't worry, I'll look after you. Then I raised my eyes a foot or so higher and gazed in awe at Lakhi's mighty and majestic lines. Kanchen was like a big fat mother as she stretched out her trunk and removed some branches that had become entangled in her younger companion's large ears. You could watch elephants for ever, I thought.

It seemed that Parbati had also read my mind.

'See,' she said, 'Kanchen likes you. You have passed most important test. You must love her well. She must know your voice, your smell. Every day, between 1 p.m. and 4 p.m. you will spend with her – talking, feeding, touching. That is most important time. And soon', she added, 'you will forget Tara.'

I laughed and turned to tell her that that was very unlikely but, again, as quickly as she had appeared, without a sound she was gone, like some strange jungle spirit.

I sat alone, watching the mahouts. From their management of the elephants, one could clearly see the difference in their characters. Phandika, the older man, was gruffer, harsher. He spat and swore as he bullied these huge creatures around as if they were children. Dino was quieter, handling Lakhi and Kanchen more gently, but still with the same firm assurance.

Physically they could not have been more different. Dino was tiny. A shock of thick black hair proudly crowned a flat wide face that was more characteristic of a Guatemalan Indian than a native of this subcontinent. Apart from a pair of broad shoulders, his slight frame belied the strength which I was to experience later. Phandika was bigger, built like an old yew tree, worn and iron hard, his arms and legs a tangle of steel-like sinew.

Despite his slightly protruding teeth and a mischievous lock of hair which permanently stood erect, like a cock's comb, from the top of his snowy white head, he was a handsome man. As I was soon to discover, he was also cunning. His eyes gave him away. He resembled an old fox.

His real name, Parbati told me, was Mono. Phandika was just a nickname derived from the word *phand*, or *phandi*, which means noose or nooser, and is only bestowed on people who have successfully lassoed elephants by that most dangerous method of elephant capture – *mela shikar*. In the elephant world it is the supreme accolade – one cannot achieve higher.

Phandika also has the distinction of holding the world record in lassoing wild elephants with one hundred and fifty elephants to his own noose. For most of his life he had worked for Parbati's legendary father, Laljee Barua. Phandika had been with Parbati when, as a teenager, she had caught Lakhi, her first elephant. After her father died, Parbati told me, Phandika had become her guru. The respect in which they held each other was obvious.

It was dark by the time I returned from the pilkhana. A fire – a large one, I was glad to see – was burning cheerfully in the centre of the circle formed by the tents. There was no sign of Parbati. But Aditya was home, judging by the frequent bright explosions of light that lit up the purple frog as he tested his flashes. Somebody had been at work around the campsite. Strips of sacking had been placed neatly in front of the opening of the tents beside which little pegs had been driven into the ground.

A voice suddenly sounded from nowhere.

'For our glasses.'

Shading my eyes against the glare of the fire, I discovered Parbati sitting cross-legged and quite still, dwarfed by the massive opening of the big tent. She had been there all the while. The next time I looked up she had disappeared again. One minute she was there and the next she was gone. When she reappeared she was carrying three glasses, two of which she handed to me.

'One for Aditya and one for you. Always wash them before you sleep. Place them on pegs. Tea, milk, sugar and particularly booze', she added pointedly, 'attract snakes, ants and centipedes.'

Hearing the clink of glasses Aditya abandoned his cameras and wormed his way out of his lair, clutching a bottle of rum. He offered some to Parbati.

She shook her head. 'Only water for me. Tomorrow you start work, Mark. You will learn cooking. I will teach you jungle cooking. Roast eggs. When you go home you will be indebted to me. Your wife will be most pleased.'

I noticed the gleam of teeth in the gloom as Aditya smiled at this latest development.

Under a blue velvet sky, glittering with stars, we dined simply off large metal platters filled with rice, potatoes and wild aubergines, liberally laced with red-hot chillis. After dinner I told Parbati of our meeting with the forest officer and asked her about the electric fences.

Angry, she said, 'Bloody humbug. Electric fences do not stop elephants. They are too clever. Tusker knocks down post, stands on it and herd crosses. Or he uses tusks. Electricity cannot hurt ivory. Sometimes elephants roll underneath. Very agile. Anyway', she continued, 'electric fences do not work around here. People steal parts.'

'You mean,' I said, 'that the elephants do come through?'

'Of course, every night,' she said, 'but you will not hear them. You hear bird but not elephant. Do not worry. They are my friends. With me, you are safe. Now, let us sleep. Work starts at 5 a.m. GMT.'

I looked at my fragile little tent and thought of the hundreds of tons which would tiptoe past me in the night. Curiously I was not nervous. I knew that while I was in the presence of this strange and magical woman nothing could go wrong.

I opened the flap of Bhim's old tent, expecting to be assailed by his odours. To my astonishment, I found a small bowl from which a cloud of burning incense was perfuming my tent. 'Mosquitoes,' a voice pierced the dark. And I fell asleep as the scented smoke carried away the spirit of the old mahout.

4
Concentration Camp

A dull thud close to my left ear rudely awakened me. I sat bolt upright in the darkness, disoriented, unsure of my whereabouts. The evocative sounds of rural India awakening carried softly through the cold morning air – the urgent crow of a cock in a distant village, the murmur of the mahouts and the familiar puffing, rumbling, squeaking, crunching and munching as eight tons of elephants started their breakfast. I relaxed and sighed happily. Plumping up my nice white British Airways pillow, I went back to sleep.

A few minutes later there came a sharp crack. A small pebble hummed through the air, two inches above my nose and ricocheted off the aluminium pole at the back of the tent. Furious, I scrambled out of the tent.

'What the . . .'

'Good morning, Mark,' a disembodied voice announced in the darkness. 'It is 5.07 a.m. You are late. First duty of chaarkatiyas is to fetch water from river to make tea. Phandika will give you bucket.'

Focusing my eyes, I found Parbati sitting cross-legged, nonchalantly dangling from her fingers a small wooden catapult. Her ammunition lay in a neat pile beside her.

'You might have hit me,' I said crossly.

'I never miss. Now go and fetch water.'

Phandika and Dino greeted me enthusiastically and gave me

three buckets. As I stomped towards the river a familiar sleepy voice called out.

'Hey, chai-wallah! Make sure the water's clean. I'll have two sugars.'

Angry, I waded into the icy torrent and immediately lost my footing, my soft feet skidding on the smooth surface of the many boulders that littered the riverbed. I fell into the freezing water, losing my grip on the buckets. As I thrashed around I saw them bobbing away. I was saved from further damage and humiliation by the arrival of Dino. Agile as a monkey, he danced across the stones, picked me up, slung me across his shoulder and carried me back to the bank. He quickly retrieved the buckets. I thanked him, at the same time checking over his shoulder to see if anybody had witnessed my Clouseau-like debut. A look of amusement was creasing Phandika's worn face as he crouched over the fire and I marched back with two full buckets. Dino, with natural good manners and kindness, a welcome trait in this sweatshop of hell, had chivalrously carried the other.

Perhaps the old fox possessed a soft spot too. He offered to make the tea. More likely I was not yet to be trusted with this most important ritual of everyday Indian life.

I glanced at my watch. It was only 5.45 a.m. I had been awake precisely 42 minutes. Already I felt as if I had run a marathon. I thought back wistfully to those days on the road with Tara – bed-tea and biscuits served by Bhim at 7 a.m. followed by a leisurely breakfast. By the time Aditya and I had washed, Tara would have been fed, watered and fully saddled and we would simply climb on board and plod off into the cool of the morning.

'Nice bath?' Aditya remarked through the opening of his tent as he lay cocooned in the cosy bundle of his down sleeping-bag while I tried to slip past to change my soaking clothes. At least Parbati had not noticed. The flap of her tent was closed.

I changed into a dry T-shirt and lungi and then sat outside my tent to await further orders. It was just beginning to get light. In the distance Kanchenjunga was awakening and chilled us with an icy kiss, languidly throwing back her lacy shawls as the wisps of cloud slowly dissipated to reveal her diamond crown, like some beautiful virgin queen – high, imperious and untouchable.

At 28,168 feet, she is the third highest mountain in the world and remained unviolated until a British expedition reached the top in 1955. Respectful of local beliefs, the team did not step on to the actual summit, considered sacrosanct and steeped in legend. According to Major L. A. Waddle, in his book *Among the Himalayas*, the name Kanchenjunga is Tibetan, and literally means 'the five repositories of the great glaciers . . . The loftiest crest, which was most conspicuously gilded by the rising and setting sun, was made the treasury of gold; the southern peak which remained in cold, grey shade until it whitened in the rising sunlight, was made the treasury of silver and the remaining peaks were named, respectively the treasures of gems, grain and holy books – the chief objects worth treasuring in the opinion of the religious Tibetans.'

It was a queen of a more mortal kind who put the fear of God into me that morning as she appeared suddenly from her tent. I jumped to my feet and stared in astonishment. The transformation was remarkable. The beige silk mekla had been replaced by a pair of faded jeans and a loose-fitting combat jacket fastened with shiny brass buttons. Her lustrous mass of thick hair had been drawn tightly back and stuffed into an old jungle hat, set at a jaunty angle. Those unsettling eyes were camouflaged by a pair of very dark sunglasses.

Hanging low on either side of her hips, like a pair of six-shooters, hung her kukris, long curved knives housed in two scabbards that were beautifully carved with flowers and elephants. She looked like a small, deadly gunslinger. Taking an oblong silver canister from her pocket, she removed the lid, deftly tipped some chewing tobacco into the palm of her hand, rolled it into a small ball and popped it into the corner of her mouth.

'Come,' she said, 'I want to show you something.'

We walked across the damp meadow towards the electric fence. At intervals she would squat down and study the ground.

'Elephants come through here,' she said, pointing to an area just under the electric fence about fifty yards from our tents.

'And,' she continued as we retraced our steps, 'move this way. Five females and three calves.'

'They came past here last night?' I stammered, assessing the distance between my tent and where we were standing. 'Come on, Parbati, you're joking. I can't see anything.'

'You would not. You do not know what to look for.'

I followed her towards the thick privet hedge that bordered our camp. A huge hole had been smashed through it.

I was still sceptical. 'That could have been done ages ago.'

'And this?' she said, looking down at a large pile of elephant dung. She broke the crust off with her foot. A small plume of steam rose up from its moist centre emitting a pleasant smell, not unlike wet hay. 'About three hours now, Mark,' she stated. 'Next job is to clean pilkhana.'

A. J. W. Milroy who was Deputy Conservator of forests in Assam produced a treatise on elephant management in 1922 in which he claimed:

It is safe to say that only the most exceptional mahout (such as most of us can never hope to meet) can be trusted to keep a pilkhana even reasonably clean without supervision, and it is well known that many men, who will do all they ought to do without any trouble so long as they fear surprise visits from authority, prove thoroughly lazy and unreliable as soon as no check is kept on their work.

Parbati was not taking any chances either. Like a small bird of prey, she perched on a stump overlooking the pilkhana, her dark eyes unfathomable behind those black glasses.

Milroy also wrote: 'The elephant's motto is "all time is lost wot is not spent in eating".' I agreed with these pearls of wisdom as I viewed the immense piles of dung, branches and slimy segments of stripped banana stems that rose like small hillocks around me. I had come all this way to learn about elephants and was ending up as a lavatory attendant.

Two hours later Parbati was satisfied. She should have been. The pilkhana resembled the centre court at Wimbledon. I collapsed on the bank next to Aditya, exhausted, sweaty and stinking – my hands a patchwork of tiny cuts.

'That, my friend,' he spluttered, 'was the most enjoyable two hours I have ever spent in my life. After this, you can get a job with me any time – as my sweeper.'

I made my way slowly towards the river. Earlier that morning I had cursed its icy torrents, but now I embraced its solace and beauty, enhanced by the arrival of the sun. I had just reached the bank when a voice rang out.

'Where are you going, Mark?'

'Just to have a wash, Parbati.'

'Well do not be long. Dusting begins in ten minutes.'

Dusting! One minute a lavatory attendant, the next a house-maid. What bloody next? I looked down at my watch. It was only eight o'clock.

Dusting did not involve cleaning out the cobwebs in the vaulted corners of Parbati's tent. Instead, I was given a piece of sackcloth and ordered to bash the hell out of Kanchen to remove the dust that elephants chuck over themselves to cool down and protect their skin from insects.

Fondly I remembered Tara's chaarkatiya's idea of dusting – a quick five-minute brush up before moving off – as I, now invisible in a thick cloud of dust, swung the heavy sackcloth wearily again and again against the mountain of skin in front of me.

As the dirt slowly fell away and two large molehills began to resemble elephants, I now realised my first impression of Lakhi and Kanchen was a little out of line. I was finding out how well maintained they really were. They had to be – Parbati and her mahouts' livelihood depended on them.

Compared to Kanchen and Lakhi, Tara was a pampered princess – and I wondered idly what would happen if they met. Tara, who I think was a bit of a snob, would probably have looked down that long nose of hers at these two bits of rough trade but, I mused, it might do her some good to mingle with the working classes and . . .

'Mark!' A sharp voice about fifteen feet above me interrupted my reverie. 'Stop dreaming. Keep dusting.'

44

I looked up to find Parbati lying between Lakhi's ears, decorating her forehead in a delicate fringe of pearls with a piece of white chalk. When she had finished, she stood up and sashayed like a trapeze artist along Lakhi's back. She paused and stood with her arms crossed until Lakhi had obediently lowered her left leg, then stepped daintily to the ground. It was beautiful to watch.

Parbati, I noticed, had changed her clothes. The gunslinger's outfit had been replaced by a T-shirt and a red and purple lungi. A yellow *gumcha*, or towel, was knotted around her head. The sunglasses had gone and so had one of her six-shooters. Only one kukri rested menacingly on her hip. She now resembled a pirate.

She walked slowly around Kanchen, who was kneeling patiently on the ground, and inspected her. I held my breath.

'First class,' she said and patted me on the back.

I could not believe it. A compliment.

'Now make Kanchen beautiful,' she added as she threw me a piece of chalk.

Art had never been my *metier*. I could not even draw a straight line.

'I'm not too good at this sort of thing, Parbati,' I stammered.

'It does not matter. You will do your level best.'

While Parbati wandered off towards the tents, I walked around in front of Kanchen. She gave me a suspicious look. Holding her left ear I stepped nervously in between her great bent knees and set to work. Kanchen shook her head and the chalk flew out of my hand. I picked it up and started again. Exactly the same thing happened.

It was then that Phandika, who was sitting astride her neck, growled a command. Kanchen picked up the piece of chalk in the tip of her trunk and passed it to the old man.

'Smoke,' he demanded, his eyes glinting.

I smiled. Bribery. This was more like it. I handed him a cigarette which disappeared into the folds of his lungi. He peered round to see if the coast was clear and then, leaning down, completed the job with a few deft strokes. He winked at me. I had found an ally and broken down another barrier.

45

Parbati returned and studied Phandika's handiwork. She smiled knowingly.

'Good. Now every day you will decorate both elephants. Come, it is time to collect fodder. We go into forest on elephants.'

At last I had a chance to impress her. I dashed round in front of Kanchen, grabbed both her ears, placed my foot on her trunk and yelled 'Utha, utha.' Nothing happened. She stood there looking slightly amazed.

'What are you doing, Mark?' Parbati asked, equally amazed.

'Well, getting on, or trying to get on Kanchen,' I replied. 'You said we were going to the forest on the elephants.'

'You are not mahout,' she stated. You are chaarkatiya. Chaarkatiya sits on back of elephant. Behind mahout. Phandika will ride Kanchen.'

I started to become angry. 'Look, Parbati. I know I'm a beginner but I have ridden Tara eight hundred miles across India . . .'

She interrupted me. 'Sometimes, Mark, it takes five years to become mahout.'

I slunk around behind Kanchen who was now sitting. Dino stood holding her tail which he had curled into a loop to form a step. I was being treated like a geriatric. Crossly I put my foot into the loop and climbed up on to Kanchen's back.

My anger subsided as we crossed the Murti. I watched with pleasure as these two titans picked their way through the minefield of boulders, sweeping their trunks in front of them through the water like metal detectors. There is a common belief that elephants are clumsy and noisy. This is a fallacy. Unlike a horse, they hardly ever stumble and on several occasions I have found myself surrounded in a forest by an entire herd. I just had not heard them.

We entered a strip of forest. 'Parbati, is . . . ?'

'Be quiet, Mark. Enjoy this forest,' she said softly. 'It will not last long.'

I concentrated on the back of Phandika's neck. Sometimes he would growl to Kanchen – that strange unintelligible language only understood by the mahout and his elephant. Unlike Tara, who wandered and stopped at will, these elephants were like well-oiled machines. They kept a steady but quick shuffling gait and my spine, buttocks and, particularly the insides of my thighs, forced apart across Kanchen's broad back, were beginning to feel the strain. Occasionally I would sneak a glance at Parbati. She sat, straight as the stem of a lotus flower, on Lakhi's broad shoulders, rocking gently, rider and elephant moving as one.

To this day I am still unsure what prompted the following incident – whether a hidden signal from Parbati, or Kanchen was genuinely spooked – for suddenly, without warning, she took off. Elephants over a short distance can achieve speeds of up to twenty miles an hour, and as I felt Kanchen accelerate away I knew I was going to fall off. I grabbed hold of Phandika's lungi as I slid down her right flank. I slid further. My head was now hanging below her belly and her pounding feet rushed up towards me. All at once, like a bungee jumper, I was catapulted on to Kanchen's back again. I recovered my composure.

'Wild elephants', Parbati said with the ghost of a smile flitting across her face, 'frightened my sweeties.'

We stopped in a sunny clearing surrounded by tall bud and peepul trees. The thickest branches were clustered together at the tops of the trees. A smooth expanse of bark, like a telegraph-pole, soared upwards. I was a good climber but this was way out of my league. Parbati sensed my nervousness.

'Poni and Babul will climb and cut fodder. Just watch and learn.'

While we waited for the boys, Parbati let Kanchen and Lakhi roam. 'Come,' she said, 'I will show you something.'

It was very still. A few gorgeous butterflies floated among the foliage – even the endless whine of the cicadas had ceased.

'Watch Lakhi and Kanchen carefully,' Parbati said quietly. As carefully as I could, I watched two elephants engage in their favourite occupation.

'They're eating,' I said.

'They are eating, Mark, but they are looking and choosing what they eat. See . . .'

I watched Kanchen push her trunk into the centre of a large bush. Looking more closely, I saw that she had parted the foliage as though searching for something. From among the leaves she extricated the berries of a small plant and popped them into her mouth.

'That is for digestion.'

'You mean,' I said, 'the elephants show you the medicine they need?'

'Of course. Sometimes we would be in jungle for nine months. There are no doctors in jungle. We learn about different plants that help elephants. When we see elephant suffer from bad stomach, we let it loose. The elephant goes where it wants, finds right plant. We collected these plants and send to specialists in Calcutta to be analysed. When we receive results, we then decide proper dose. That is how we learn to treat our elephants.'

I marvelled at this harmonious arrangement.

'My papa taught me all of these things. These forests are like medicine boxes. Not only for animals but for people. But for how long? People destroy everything. They do not realise what they are losing,' she said sadly.

It was the first time I had seen Parbati genuinely upset. She looked like a lost child.

'I will teach you what I can, Mark. It is most important you tell people, all people, what they are destroying. By hurting our forests, they are hurting themselves, our elephants and all animals.' She stooped down to pluck a few stems of a small and delicate fern.

'What are those,' I asked, 'more medicine?'

She shook her head. 'No. For dinner.'

We walked slowly back, comfortable in our silence. I was beginning to feel at ease with this remarkable woman. Surrounded by the beauty and quietness of the forest and her elephants, she was relaxed. It was not surprising. This was her home.

High in the treetops, Poni and Babul were hard at work cutting fodder, the sun flashing off their blades. Every now and again they shouted a warning as a huge branch crashed to the ground. Following instructions from Phandika and Dino standing on their backs, the elephants would pick up the food in their trunks and pass it back to be stacked in neat piles.

I watched them work and wondered at the rapport between this great beast and man in this most bizarre and ancient of relationships – a relationship in which the elephant could so easily kill his keeper but instead becomes his best friend. In Sanskrit the elephant is known as *mrigahastin* – the beast with one hand. Its trunk is powered by a hundred thousand muscles and combines awesome strength with great dexterity. With it an elephant can easily uproot a tree or remove a pip from an orange. Its sneeze can even knock out a dog.

Two hours later, our task was completed. Parbati broke into song. Serenaded by her clear bell-like voice, perched high like maharajahs on giant howdahs of emerald green, we rode majestically home with a day's food for two elephants.

5
Of Gurus and Ghosts

We reached camp and unloaded the fodder. I glanced at my watch. It was just before noon – lunchtime. Unfortunately, around here elephants came first, and what was worse they were fed by hand.

Compared to my next job, I would gladly have shovelled elephant shit all day. Parbati and I sat cross-legged in front of two large bowls – one full of wheat, the other black rock-salt. Behind us lay a mountain of neatly stacked banana leaves.

'Now Mark,' she said, 'watch carefully. You will enjoy.'

Not in a million years, I thought while concentrating on her deft handiwork. Picking up a banana stalk, she tore the leaf in half lengthways like a sheet of paper. She then spread it in front of her and, after scoring the thick stem in three places, neatly folded the sections on top of one another. From the bowls she added a handful of wheat and a pinch of salt. She then rolled it tightly and secured it with a stray frond. The end product resembled one of those delicious seaweed rolls that one is served in a sushi bar, but on a larger scale. They are known locally as *danas*.

'What's the salt for?' I enquired, desperately buying time to avoid this hideous version of jungle-style tatting.

'For digestion. Salt is essential for all wild animals,' she replied. 'Domesticated elephants cannot get salt. In the wild there are natural salt-licks. If you want to see animal, find a salt-lick. Every kind will be there.'

'And the wheat?'

'Wheat is also good for stomach. And this' – she held up a familiar brown substance, gur or jaggery – 'this is my treat for my sweeties . . . Now Mark, get working.'

Twenty minutes later, my fingers stuck together with the sticky white gum that oozed from the banana stems and my hands contorted like claws from cramp, I produced my first dana. I placed it reverently next to Parbati's huge pile. Compared to hers, mine resembled a straw hat that had been savaged by a puppy. No elephant could possibly be tempted by it.

Parbati surveyed my handiwork. 'You're new to it, Mark.' She gave me the kind of weary look that a teacher might give to a stupid child. 'Now I will leave you. I have other duties. Practice makes perfect.' Patting me encouragingly, she wandered off.

For the next two hours I sat, like a fat and clumsy Buddha, cursing as I fumbled my way through the pile of banana leaves. Eventually I finished and lay back exhausted. Beside me stood a pile not unlike the one I had cleared up earlier that day in the pilkhana.

My short reverie was curtailed by Phandika who, with a chuckle, dumped another mountain of leaves beside me.

'Smoke, sahib?'

Salvation, I thought, and quickly handed him two cigarettes. Tucking one behind his ear and the other in his lungi he ambled away. Bloody traitor, I muttered and, pulling my fingers apart, I continued my chores.

Lunch was a hastily eaten bowl of rice, potatoes and some unrecognisable vegetable which tasted like blotting paper.

'How's your day been?' Aditya asked, stretched out comfortably in the purple glow of the frog.

I grunted and wolfed more rice down my throat.

'Aaah,' he yawned, 'mine has been quite marvellous. I arose leisurely at eight, had a delicious breakfast and then wandered down to the river to enjoy a long and invigorating bath. Then,' he continued, drawing on his cigarette before flicking it casually towards the still-smouldering fire, 'I . . .'

'Aditya!' a voice echoed sharply from the confines of the large tent. 'Pick that up!'

Quickly Aditya rose to his feet, limped over to the fire and picked up the cigarette butt. 'How the hell did she see that?' he said softly to me. 'Her tent is closed. It's like having the Gestapo round here. But don't worry, my friend,' he whispered, 'there's an old Hindi saying: "A man at sixty is a young elephant, a woman at twenty is growing old." In the end we are the ones that are in control.'

'What did you say, Aditya?' the voice from the gloom echoed with increasing menace.

'Nothing, Parbati,' he exclaimed in astonishment. 'Just discussing wildlife.'

We now understood that we were not in the presence of any normal mortal. She was a child of nature – all her senses, but particularly her intuition, had been honed to perfection by the long years spent deep in the forests.

In the pilkhana Kanchen and Lakhi stood impatiently in front of three gunny bags beside which lay the danas, neatly divided into two piles.

'Feeding time,' Parbati announced. 'Sit there.' She pointed to the gunny bag which lay in front of Kanchen's two huge legs. Kanchen loomed above me, her pale eyes looking longingly over my shoulder. In a flash she reached over, unfurling her long proboscis, and deftly extricated five danas from the top of the pile. Parbati rapped her hard on the end of her trunk, uttering a string of unintelligible words which were clearly not of praise.

'Kanchen is greedy elephant. You must give one by one.'

I was delighted, and saw that, like Tara, the way to Kanchen's heart was through her stomach.

'During feeding you must talk to her,' Parbati continued. 'She will soon learn your voice.'

The inevitable crowd had assembled, drawn by the spectacle of this absurd foreigner squatting uncomfortably on a mat in front of an elephant. It was awkward enough, but the thought of talking to Kanchen in front of both crowd and camera was downright embarrassing. I looked to my left. Poni and Babul, already seasoned chaarkatiyas, were chatting among themselves as they fed Lakhi. What on earth do I say to this elephant? Then I had a brilliant idea – I would sing. I broke into a mournful rendition of *The Lord is My Shepherd*, a suitable choice considering my situation. Parbati was delighted.

'Good, good. Singing is good. I sang to Lakhi for sixteen hours after I caught her.'

'What happened when you . . .?'

'Do not ask so many questions, Mark,' she said impatiently. 'You will know everything in course of time. Concentrate on Kanchen.'

In the next two hours two very different characters were revealed. Kanchen was an immensely greedy elephant. I scarcely had time to reach behind me for one dana before her trunk was waving in front of my face demanding the next. I became like a conveyor belt. Finally, to save time, I gave her three at once. Her greed did not end there. Once she had finished her own, she tried to steal from Lakhi's pile.

Lakhi, on the other hand, was very fastidious – almost suspicious. After taking a dana from Poni or Babul, she would first unwrap it, check the contents and only when completely satisfied would she slowly chew it. Like a spoilt child, she would often hurl one away in a fit of rage. This behaviour might have been due to her age – she was relatively young, only twenty-five – whereas Kanchen was at least ten years her senior. I could see she was a fickle elephant. Unless one was very experienced, she would be difficult to handle. As I studied the matronly figure that stood in front of me, I was glad that it was Kanchen Parbati had chosen to become my partner. I was convinced that in the course of time, we would become firm friends.

'Listen,' Parbati said, squatting down beside me as Kanchen emitted a deep, almost inaudible rumble. 'She is talking to you. When I was tiny child, I sit everyday like you with mahouts in papa's pilkhana. There were many elephants and many mahouts. One elephant was blind. Every day I sang, I talked, I fed this elephant. Then I go back to school. When I return six months later, I came straight to pilkhana. I did not utter word. Again there were many mahouts. Immediately she picked up small stick and threw it into my lap. I was so happy. Remember Mark, elephants are pure. Open your mind and your heart to them and you will not go wrong.'

Somehow I doubted that I would ever reach this level of empathy. Still, it was encouraging, and opening my mind and my mouth I uttered another hoarse recital of *The Lord is My Shepherd*. Fifty renderings and four hundred danas later, feeding was at last over.

The sun was still high and had warmed the chill waters of the Murti enough for Kanchen and Lakhi to be taken for their daily bath. Unlike their wild brothers and sisters, domesticated working elephants cannot afford the luxury of choosing the time of day for their bath. Since an elephant must spend at least two hours in the water, it is important to ensure that the temperature of the water is correct. Like most human beings, elephants do not enjoy cold baths – and, like us, they are susceptible to even the common cold.

For me this is the most enjoyable part of looking after an elephant. It is simply enormous fun. Eagerly, I grabbed one of the pumice stones and rushed in to join Phandika who was vigorously scrubbing Kanchen's vast expanse of flesh as she lay peacefully on her side in the water.

'Do not', a familiar voice barked out from the bank, 'approach Kanchen from front. She does not know you well enough yet. Come from back.'

It was too late. The sight of this foreigner, clad only in a wet lungi, was clearly too much for the elephant. Rolling backwards to gain momentum, she lumbered to her feet, dislodging Phandika into the icy river. Phandika, like all mahouts, regarded cleaning an elephant as just another daily chore, which does not necessarily involve getting wet. He glowered at me and ordered Kanchen back into the water. I smiled innocently. I had now paid him back. We were even.

I set about my immense task in some trepidation. Soon my arms were aching with fatigue and I could hardly hold the stone.

'One hour one side. One hour the other,' Parbati announced,

wading through the water towards me, her lungi hitched up to her knee, which although totally respectable by western standards, would have raised eyebrows and even registered shock in traditional India.

'Washing elephants, Mark,' she rebuked me, 'is not game. First we check their condition for wounds and for things like this. She stooped down and removed a large leech hidden in the soft downy hair inside Kanchen's ear. She pinched it quickly between her thumbnail and forefinger. I watched in fascination as bright red blood erupted into her palm. She threw the remains of the leech into the river, washed her hand and moved around Kanchen. Squatting down in the water, she lifted one of the huge front legs into her lap and began to tap the scarred and pitted sole of the foot. I held my breath. I knew from experience how ticklish elephants were. In a similar situation Tara had once displayed her sensitivity by kicking me in the stomach.

I couldn't help myself. 'Be careful, Parbati. You know how ticklish . . .'

'Ticklish?' she retorted. 'Of course they are not ticklish. I'm checking her feet for disease – we call it *kari*. Come!' She noticed my hesitation. 'Do not worry. I am here. She will not harm you.'

I squatted down beside her.

'See. Kanchen's sole is good. It is not soft. If kari is here, Kanchen's foot would be soft.' She checked the other feet. 'Kari is dangerous,' she continued. 'If not cured quickly, elephant cannot work, she is useless. Sometimes,' she added, 'you can detect kari if elephant is not sure-footed. They will go slowly, particularly over sharp stones.'

My stomach tightened on hearing this. I remembered how cautious and slow Tara had been on rocky paths and how, when I urged her on, she would place little stones on her head to explain the problem. I had thought she was just being lazy.

Parbati noticed my consternation. 'What is wrong?'

I told her about Tara.

'That was four years ago. If Tara had kari she would not be able to walk at all. See,' she smiled, 'you are already learning so much. Now when you go back you will look after her properly.'

We watched in silence as the two elephants, their baths finished, rose majestically out of the water and stood drying in the evening sunshine, glistening like two heaps of wet coal.

'They are bigger than us, are they not?' Parbati suddenly remarked.

'Well . . . yes . . . they are,' I answered, perplexed.

'But not few minutes ago?'

'No,' I answered, not really seeing where this conversation was leading.

'Bathing is only time when we little people are bigger. Elephants are vulnerable when lying down. They learn to trust you. Bathing is as important as feeding. Think about it. Now,' she said, 'your duties are nearly finished.'

I glanced at my watch. It was five o'clock. I made a quick calculation. I had now been on the go for twelve hours.

'Soon you will not need your watch. Soon your guide will be the sun, the moon, the stars, the clouds, Now,' Parbati said kindly, 'you have done well. Go with Phandika and Dino and settle my sweeties for night. I will meet you at campfire – then we can relax.'

I walked slowly behind Kanchen and Dino. Phandika broke into song, his rough old voice coarse but strangely haunting as it cut through the still air like a rusty saw. I found myself joining in. I had no idea of the words, but it did not seem to matter. They both turned from their lofty height and smiled down at me.

Back in the pilkhana my fellow chaarkatiyas had divided the fodder. Two large piles lay stacked, ready for some serious eating which would continue through the night. I was surprised to see that the elephants' back legs were only secured by their chains attached to small wooden stakes. Tara would have pulled these out in a second and wandered off to enjoy the fruits of some unfortunate villager's field.

It was dark when I returned from washing in the river. A large fire blazed brightly, creating an intimate atmosphere in the circumference of our tents. It was like a secret little world. In the background the evening meal was being prepared, and the low murmur of mahouts intermingled with the clatter of pots. Overhead a tiny crescent moon hung like a toy as though suspended by hidden strings.

Aditya lay sprawled outside his tent, holding a glass of rum and dressed in a snow-white ensemble of Kurta pyjamas and a thick white shawl. He looked like Father Christmas.

'Enjoying yourself?' I asked.

He grunted and slowly massaged his bad leg. It was then that I looked at his face – it was as pale as his shawl, and screwed up in agony. Selfishly immersed in my new role, I had forgotten about Aditya's hideous injury. Not only had I dragged him around taking photographs, he had once again been forced to take the role as negotiator between East and West, not just for the film crew but also between Parbati and myself. But, true to his character, he had not complained.

'Drink?' he said, his eyes twinkling, raising his glass in my direction.

I filled my glass and collapsed in a heap outside my tent.

'Where's Parbati?'

'I am here, Mark.'

I nearly jumped out of my skin. Again I had not noticed her. She was sitting in the opening of her tent, gracefully combing the mass of thick black hair that lay behind her like another small tent.

Dinner soon arrived, courtesy of Phandika, whose expertise I discovered was not confined to elephants. We dined silently, as is the custom in India, on grilled fresh-water shrimps.

*

That night we talked of many things – of men, mahouts, movies and magic. There had really only been one man in Parbati's life – her father. When she talked about him her eyes softened and her voice became childlike. Nobody, she told us could ever fill his shoes – he was father, guru and friend. She did not know why he had chosen her to continue his work; perhaps it was instinct.

Her mother, meanwhile, had been anxious for Parbati to obtain a normal education. When she was fourteen, she was sent to college, but at every given opportunity, and mostly stolen ones, she would sneak away and join her father in his jungle camps. On graduation, she presented her certificate to her mother and said, 'I have done this for you. Now let me get back to my world – back to the jungle. Back to elephants.'

Her true graduation, she said, was when her father considered her worthy of these noble beasts. Instead of a certificate he gave her a pair of metal tongs, for extracting hot coals from campfires, a gunny sack, and a little brass vessel with a spout. 'Now you are ready my girl,' he had said. 'Go out into the world. It is yours.'

I was curious about this brass vessel which she now held in her hands, caressing it fondly like a magician with a lamp. It seemed to have a life of its own and glowed ethereally in the gloom.

Parbati noticed my interest. 'This is *kamandalu*,' she explained. 'One day I will tell you strange tale.'

For the rest of the journey that vessel stuck in my mind. I felt it contained some secret, but it would be many weeks before I unravelled the mystery.

We talked of films, but not about the one we were making. Parbati's favourites were westerns and war epics, but particularly westerns – *The Magnificent Seven, High Noon, How the West Was Won*. She loved the cowboys – their rough and tumble gypsy way of life, the campfires, the gun-fights and above all the wide open spaces of the country. Charles Bronson was her favourite actor, she said. He reminded her of a tribal chief – proud and dignified. His face looked as if it had been hewn from stone. If she went to America, she told us, she would not visit the tourist sights – all she wanted to do was to sit with Charles Bronson in one of those rusty old *cantinas* and down tequilas. But unlike the heroes who act out their fantasies on the silver screen, Parbati herself was the real thing. While I stared at this exquisite and strange woman sitting demurely in the glitter of the firelight I wondered again how, as a woman, let alone a teenager, she could have survived the rough and tumble of lassoing wild elephants – the proof of which was now eating noisily in the pilkhana.

As though reading my mind she interrupted my thoughts. 'Mela shikar, Mark, is dangerous. I have seen many men killed.

Broken. One man I remember – elephant knelt and crushed him. We never found head.'

I shivered. 'But how did *you* survive?' I asked.

'Not only me, but Phandika also,' she answered slowly, a strange look coming into her eye. 'We respected spirits, obeyed rules and were protected by *Pugli Sahan*.'

'Who is Pugli Sahan?' I asked.

'Spirit.'

'A spirit?' Aditya asked.

'Spirit that must be obeyed,' Parbati announced firmly. 'I have seen her.'

It was then that she talked about magic. We listened spellbound, the cold kiss of goosebumps creeping up our backs.

She told us about one time when they were sitting around the campfire, deep in the forests. They had been there for about two months but had failed to catch any elephants. That night it was raining and the trees were full of mist. Suddenly they heard a clapping sound. A young girl appeared wearing a beautiful white sari. Her long black hair fell to her waist and she was smiling. The rain seemed to part over her head and she remained dry. Thinking she was lost, they welcomed her and bade her into the camp, but she did not move. Becoming concerned, Parbati approached the apparition, carrying rice and some burning embers in a dish. But a force stopped her and she left the dish on the ground. She was not afraid.

She knew this was Pugli. Her father and Phandika had often talked about this spirit. So Parbati made her obeisance and returned to the camp. Suddenly, Pugli sat down and threw a handful of rice on to the dish of burning embers, but the rice did not burn. For a long time she stared into the embers moving the rice around with a little stick. Then she stood up. Smiling, the spirit raised four fingers and moved away. Then she clapped her hands, made a strange hooting sound and was gone.

'Immediately we were surrounded by sound of elephants,' Parbati said, 'feeding, trumpeting and breaking branches. Next morning, we caught four elephants easy as pie. Later we found that no other phandis had caught elephants.'

When they returned home, Parbati excitedly told her father what had happened. Her father and Phandika said they had seen Pugli many times. Each time the same thing had happened. However many fingers Pugli held up, they always caught that exact number of elephants.

Parbati told us Pugli has great power and must not be offended. Some mahouts and phandis had scorned the legend of Pugli. These people did not survive. A massive elephant with *tal-betal* tusks – one raised upwards, the other downwards – came and killed such men. 'It is said,' Parbati whispered, 'that Pugli sleeps on tusks of this elephant.'

I shivered and glanced at Aditya – an unsmoked cigarette, its long ash intact, lay between his fingers.

It was quiet. The fire had nearly died – just a few small flames licked hungrily round the glowing embers, throwing a strange configuration of shadows that danced eerily, like spirits, around us. I glanced across at Parbati. She was so still, only the flash of gold from her wrist bangles signalling her presence. I crawled into my tent. A few minutes later I heard the familiar clink of glass. Aditya, it seemed, was taking comfort from a small nightcap. I fell into an uneasy sleep.

*

I was awoken from my nightmares by the sound of a pitched battle. In panic I crawled out of my tent to find Parbati sitting by the dying fire.

'Elephants have come,' she said quietly. 'Look.'

The skyline was lit up like a fireworks display. The golden tracers of rockets arced gracefully across the sky, exploding in a flash of silver stars. I could hear the sound of panicked voices as the villagers fought to defend their crops from the marauding and starving elephants. It was obviously a battle fought at close quarters for, amid all the hullabaloo, I could make out the guttural bellow of frightened calves and the shrill trumpet of enraged mothers as they too mustered their troops. Parbati seemed quite unmoved.

She shrugged her shoulders. 'Harvesting has begun. Every

night elephants will come now. They are hungry. They have no home, no food, no forests. They have to eat or they will starve. And each night there will be death. Elephants will die, people will die.' She wrung her hands together. 'What to do? What to do?' she breathed, and disappeared into her tent.

6

Driving Lessons

Over the next week or so life in the concentration camp
continued much as before. My routine rarely varied except
for the dana making. Parbati quite rightly pointed out that I took
so long, and the end product was so poor, that the elephants would
starve if I continued.

In spite of this I was beginning to regain confidence. Although
Parbati still scolded me when I made mistakes and checked my
work diligently, I felt I was making progress. Little by little, as
she and her mahouts encouraged and sometimes even praised
me, I felt myself becoming part of their world. Gradually the
habits and formality of my western side began to slip away. Well,
some of them did . . .

Parbati did not like toothpaste. In the morning she simply
scooped up the cold ashes from the fire and rubbed her teeth,
assuring me it was healthier than stuff packed into tubes. She
also disliked soap. Instead she used a strange jungle formula
concocted from a mixture of water and burnt bamboo. Aditya
and I experimented with this preparation down at the river and
ended up looking like a couple of Naga sadhus. I also reneged on
the weekly full body application of mustard oil that Parbati and
the mahouts applied. It promoted, I was told, soft skin, a deep
sleep and was also a good insect repellent. Again I could not be
tempted.

Unlike the West, where the garbage bin has become a central

focus of most households, here nothing was wasted – be it a piece of string, an empty bottle or even a scrap of plastic. Everything was put to some use; sheaves of soft jute attached to a simple wooden handle became a brush for applying the dreaded mustard oil or for administering to the wounds of the elephants; the fibre from a creeper soaked in kerosene, rolled into a bundle and placed in the top of a piece of bamboo was transformed into a pretty and efficient lamp. Even Aditya had caught this ecological bug. He now went around picking up butt-ends (mostly his own) and little pieces of paper on the point of a specially designed stick, admonishing everybody with a little rhyme. 'Don't let the litter spoil the glitter.'

Now that Parbati had spared me from the time-consuming and hideous task of making the danas, I spent the afternoons getting to know the other female that dominated my life at that moment – Kanchen.

She really was the most extraordinary shape – long rather than tall, with a perfectly rounded belly that hung from her legs like a barrel. Elephants in India are classified by their build. Broadly speaking, there are two main *bands* or castes – *Koomeriah* and *Meergah*. *Koomeriahs* are short, thick beasts which are considered princely and royal; *Meergahs* are long-legged and light. The ideal combination Parbati told me is *Boormeergah* a blend of both – thus combining strength with speed. Lakhi, Parbati said, was *Boormeergah* but Kanchen did not fit into any of these categories. Apparently she was a *Shola* elephant, so named because her body resembled the shape of a local fish of similarly strange proportions.

Although Lakhi was bigger, more perfect and Parbati's favourite, I could now see that Kanchen was the boss. Lakhi was an exceedingly playful elephant and enjoyed games. Her favourite toy was a stick which she would wedge between her chin and her chest and squeeze. Inevitably it would break, and she would then look forlornly about her for another. Kanchen would rootle around in the discarded fodder until she found something similar and pass it to her. This could go on for hours. Until, fed up with her younger sister's strange quirks, she would confiscate the stick and rap Lakhi lightly on her trunk as if to say, that's enough.

Early mornings, Parbati explained, are the worst time for elephants. They have yet to be fed and are waiting for the familiar and reassuring sight of their mahout to attend to their needs. All domesticated elephants eventually replace their natural family with their mahouts and until that person whom they have come to know and trust appears before them they panic like lost children. They have to rely on these small, strange surrogates for those two most important parts of an elephant's life, food and protection.

I witnessed the most extraordinary displays of affection between Kanchen and Lakhi at this most hostile hour of the day. In a tangle of giant trunks they embraced one another like long lost lovers. Unlike Tara, an elephant on her own, Kanchen and Lakhi did at least have each other.

It was then that I thought how lonely Tara must be. She needed another elephant, to be with her, to share her everyday worries, her ways which we do not understand. I knew I must find her a companion.

Like the blind elephant that threw sticks into Parbati's lap when she returned from college, I was now getting similar recognition from Kanchen. The single act of sniping that Parbati employed with a small catapult to wake me up had now been replaced by a machine-gun as Kanchen – perhaps more concerned about food than protection – rattled the very foundations of my tent with a continuous barrage of sticks, stones and anything else she could lay her trunk on.

Parbati was delighted. 'You have made good progress, Mark. Kanchen is relying on you.'

And soon I would be relying on her, for Parbati announced that we would be starting the journey. It was time to practise riding.

The next morning she beckoned me into her tent. I had been tempted on many occasions, I admit, to pull back the mosquito net that hung tantalisingly across the entrance to what I pictured as a treasure trove. This net had assumed the mystical allure of one of those carved stone screens that one finds in old palaces protecting the women's *zenana*. Parbati could see out, as I knew only too well, but I could not see in. Fortunately Aditya had been there to remind me, rightly and somewhat acidly, that I was supposed to be a gentleman, and here, at least, in his country I was to mind my manners. So this invitation was like tasting forbidden fruit. I climbed in after carefully wiping my feet on the gunny bag lying outside.

I was not disappointed. She was like a magpie, and at that moment she did not look unlike that sharp, bright and glossy thief as she sat in the centre of her nest surrounded by an amazing cornucopia of bits and pieces, holding three or four bright safety-pins between her teeth. She grunted something and flew off quickly, alighting among a pile of boxes that were neatly stacked in a far corner of the tent. While she rustled about it gave me an opportunity to have a look around.

Her bedding was simple – three thin and threadbare mattresses stacked on top of one another, placed exactly in the centre of the tent. There was no pillow. Her two immense grey suitcases lay at the foot of the bed. One was thrown open and from it a dazzling array of clothing exploded haphazardly in a blaze of colour. The other was closed – silent and forbidding as a tomb. On top of this vinyl mausoleum lay three objects – a bright red comb, a pot of cream, and in a small frame a black and white photograph. It portrayed a short young man, dressed in a khaki shirt and matching half-pants, his legs encased in puttees. His feet were bare. It was the eyes which gave him away. It was Laljee Barua, Parbati's father.

In the corners of the tent, on hooks fashioned from elephant shackles, hung clusters of small exquisite rattan baskets like bunches of dried fruit. Next to these hung her weapons – five or six kukris of different shapes and lengths sheathed snugly in carved scabbards. Below them, stretching along the entire length of the tent, were spare ropes, chains and a bewildering array of hand-forged tools. In another corner, nestling in a small cardboard box, were a selection of small round bottles with glass stoppers, the contents of each neatly labelled in some unintelligible script. And in the other corner, standing by itself, my eye caught the dull glow of the little kamandalu.

Parbati had now almost disappeared into the cardboard box

in which she was burrowing like a maddened ant. She gave a triumphant grunt and extricated four soft white cotton rolls. They looked like bandages. They were. God, I thought, what next; now we're going to play at hospitals.

'Come,' she said. 'Now we ride.'

My scorn was replaced by anguish. What on earth, I thought, did bandages have to do with elephants? Surely bandages were for injury . . .

'Hurry up, Mark,' Parbati called, and I crawled outside to find her sitting on the ground – one leg and foot already encased like an Egyptian mummy, secured by one of those large safety-pins. She was beginning to bind up the other.

'Here,' she said, throwing me the bandages, 'do like me.'

'But Parbati, is this really necessary?' I asked. 'Why do I need bandages?'

'Your legs are fat and soft, Mark,' she explained. 'When new to riding elephants you need them.'

She was not going to get away with this. 'But I didn't need bandages when I rode Tara.'

She turned quickly, her eyes blazing. 'Pupils do not question gurus. Put them on.'

Half an hour later I stood up and waddled to the pilkhana like a penguin. Dino and Phandika were waiting on the elephants.

'By the way, Parbati,' I asked, 'why do *you* need them?'

'To make *you* feel better.' She ran lightly along Lakhi's long back and settled behind her ears. 'Kanchen is now yours. Phandika will be behind you and I am here. Just concentrate and enjoy.'

I grabbed Kanchen's huge ears, placed one foot on her trunk and made a silent prayer that all my hard work had paid off. She looked at me her pale eyes glowing softly and before I had a chance to utter the appropriate command I was thrown through the air. I landed in Phandika's lap and embraced him passionately.

'First class, sahib,' he said, extricating himself from my clutches and poking me in the tummy with a small wooden stick to indicate that I should turn around. I settled myself on Kanchen's shoulders. It was then that I understood why I needed bandages. Kanchen's neck was encircled tightly by a thick loop of knotted ropes, like a horse's girth. Attached to it and hanging behind Kanchen's ears were two rope stirrups.

'Put your feet under ropes and into stirrups,' Parbati shouted at me.

It was easier said than done. 'It's far too tight,' I shouted back, trying to force my legs under the girth and feeling the bandages tear against my skin.

'They are not too tight. You must get used to them.'

Sweaty and swearing, I eventually forced them through. The pressure against the side of my legs was enormous.

'Now put your feet in stirrups,' she commanded. 'I made them. Do they fit?'

'Very nicely, Parbati.' I grunted in agony. 'There is only one problem. When Kanchen raises her head I feel as if my toes are going to break.'

'That is normal,' she said. 'You will get used to it.'

By now I was blessing the bandages. Once I was settled I found them remarkably comfortable. The stirrups, however, did have to be adjusted to compensate for my height. Otherwise I would have ended up hunched like a flat-race jockey. I realised I had forgotten something and yelled at Aditya to fetch my old *ankush* which I had carried from India to England and back, just for this occasion.

'Ankush?' Parbati queried sharply. 'What ankush? On my elephants you do not use ankush. Occasionally, when in trouble, we use these.' She held up a pair of cone-shaped wooden objects with small metal tips which were attached by ropes behind Lakhi's ears. 'Lakhi is young and fickle,' she explained, 'sometimes she needs discipline. Even then I do not use. She feels them. That is enough. On Kanchen you will not need anything. She is good elephant. If you like you can use this.' She held up a small bamboo stick, similar to the one Phandika had used on my stomach. 'Just for tapping,' she added.

For the film, the producer wanted to show the audience back home that I had never ridden an elephant before. He assured me that a display of total incompetence would have them rolling around in their seats. I complied with his expertise and turned in a virtuoso performance, which I humbly think was deserving of an Oscar.

Although two elephants are never the same, and no animal senses lack of confidence more quickly, I soon found myself adapting to Kanchen. She really was a good elephant. Compared with Tara it was like driving a finely-tuned racing car with power steering. She was very responsive and almost anticipated my little nudges behind her ears or the commands that I shouted. Parbati smiled with approval and even Phandika, after poking me in the ribs with his stick to keep my back straight, and at the same time cunningly extracting a cigarette, grudgingly praised me.

'Shabash,' he growled, 'shabash mahout.'

But I still had a lot to learn – including a whole new vocabulary of commands. Phandika repeated them endlessly into my ear.

Jhook	– lower knees for dismounting
Doomrokh	– keep tail still
Bookkhol	– hold breath
Dumkhol	– lift tail
Thel	– push
Dake	– step over
Dekkay	– see, look
Chup	– keep silent, keep quiet
Choop	– suck, take water
Aste	– slow
Ho Aste	– dead slow
Shabash	– well done/praise
Baini	– relax

I particularly liked one – *kholkaan*, which literally means open ears. It was used to take the pressure off my toes.

Affectionately I patted Kanchen on the top of her great bristly head and whispered 'shabash, shabash' and heard her rumble softly in appreciation. I was starting to feel part of this ancient and secretive fraternity, bonded by the love of the beast that strode beneath me.

★

Reunited with Tara at Kipling Camp

Parbati introducing Mark to Kanchen and Lakhi with the old mahout Phandika

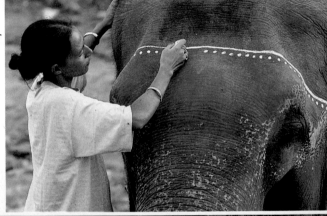

Cleaning up in the
concentration camp

First lesson in the art of
decoration

Domestic science –
Parbati shows Mark
how to make *dana* rolls
for elephants

Riding back to camp with fresh fodder

In a muddle, making the dreaded *dana* rolls

Early morning bathing

Bandaging the legs

Carrying offerings for the puja
across the river

Dino, the young mahout, watches while Parbati begins elementary driving lessons

Advanced driving lessons on a steep gradient

Right: A frightening encounter with a wild tusker

Below right: Swimming in a sea of tea

Parbati in full battle dress

Arriving at a logging camp

The Magnificent Mal Squad commanded by Captain Honeybee, (centre, in balaclava) with honorary members Mark and Aditya on the right

Last rites at the elephant grave

In India every journey or undertaking begins with a *puja*, a ceremony to invoke the blessings of the deities and to ensure good luck in the endeavour. This particular puja, Parbati explained, was something very special – a ceremony to appease and pay homage to the patron deities of the forests and elephants – an ancient tradition handed down over the centuries by the elephant catchers of Bengal and Assam. Every herd, she said, had a composition – 70 per cent belongs to the Muslim saint Mahout Pir, 15 per cent to Saatshikari, the patron goddess of the forests, 10 per cent to Mother Kali, and 5 per cent to the elephant god, Ganesh. No discrimination is made between Hindu and Muslim. Muslims pray to Hindu deities and Hindus bow down before Allah. How wonderful, I thought, that the love of elephants could unite such disparate faiths while each day dangerous sparks of religious fervour flared up in many areas of this great subcontinent.

Late in the afternoon, as the setting sun turned the surface of the river Murti gold, Phandika, Dino and I joined Parbati, who was wearing a flowing mekla the colour of a Burmese ruby, in the cool waters of the river to purify our minds, spirits and bodies. Led by Parbati, we crossed the river in procession, carrying black and white doves, chickens, sprigs of bamboo decorated with different coloured flags and little golden bowls filled with fruit, sweets and incense. As the sun dipped below the horizon and the air was perfumed by scented smoke, Parbati knelt down, her long wet hair falling like a curtain over her face, and evoked her family deities and the spirits of the forest. Then she performed the ancient puja of homage to the forests and the elephants and invoked the gods.

'We are your children. We are coming into your territory. Protect and guide us on our journey. Forgive us for our mistakes.'

*

That night, as we sat around the campfire, we were again treated to a fireworks display. This time it was closer. I could hear the rattle of chains as Lakhi and Kanchen shuffled and shifted around nervously in the pilkhana.

'The wild ones are calling them,' Parbati said.

'What do you mean?' I asked.

'No, no . . . we cannot hear it. It is too low. Scientists now say that elephants can talk to each other when many kilometres away.'

I had actually read about this somewhere. I remember feeling upset and angry. Was nothing sacrosanct any more? Mankind in its terrifying and rapacious quest for knowledge and power left no stone unturned. I felt it was a violation. It was their world not ours. Soon we might be able to understand what they were talking about. But, I mused, if it really was going to help the survival of these beautiful animals, then maybe it was worthwhile.

'Phandika!' Parbati shouted urgently, implying that something was wrong.

Aditya and I struggled to our feet.

'It is nothing,' she said. 'Lakhi has broken her chains. She is by mahouts' tent.'

Illuminated by the dying embers of the mahouts' fire Lakhi's vast shadow was just visible. Phandika emerged sleepily from his tent and led her back to the pilkhana. Aditya and I looked at one another.

'How did you know?' we both said, almost simultaneously.

Parbati shrugged. 'Feeling.'

I shivered. Even though Parbati's antennae were ultra-sophisticated, tuned to perfection, I now realised I had witnessed something else, something spooky.

'Why did Lakhi do that?' I asked.

She smiled sadly. 'Because wild ones are calling her. But Lakhi is young elephant. She is too unsure. She will not go.'

'You mean that domesticated elephants can return to the wild and be accepted by the herd?'

'Of course. Sometimes my papa lose elephants during mela shikar. Three elephants he had for twelve years disappear one day during confusion. Herd took them away. He never saw them again. But only females can go back. Herd accepts them. Males are problem. When male escape he meets other males protecting herd. They fight. He is chased out. He becomes loner, *goonda*, finding his food only among men. Then there is trouble. He kills. Then men kill him. Men,' she said, a slight smile flitting across her face, 'always problems.'

'But,' she continued, 'things have changed. In my papa's days elephants could return to wild – there was still some forest. Now it is not possible. What will happen to Kanchen and Lakhi if they go back? They will starve. Soon they will be wounded. Soon they will die, slowly. Is it not better for elephant', she said quietly, 'to have some life than no life at all? You should know – think of Tara.'

7
Death in the Night

The tranquillity of early morning tea was interrupted by the roar of a jeep. It was the District Forest Officer. He was on his way to an area about forty-five minutes away where in the early hours of the previous night a tea plucker had been killed by an elephant. He said that these tragedies were occurring more frequently and that it would be a valid and important scene to record in our film. Considering his busy and often dangerous job, it was a thoughtful gesture. We accepted gratefully. Parbati did not want to come – she had seen it all too many times before.

The film crew quickly packed the gear and we set off in the jeeps, stopping once to pick up a burly policeman who was to act as our guard. I noticed that he was wearing running shoes – not a good omen, I thought, staring down at my fragile flip-flops.

It took us hours to get there. The road had been blocked by the tea garden union – apparently a normal event on such occasions. They would not move until an acceptable compromise had been reached and compensation worked out. The trucks were backed up for miles but nobody seemed to care. Waiting is part of Indian life. People chatted, slept and played cards underneath lungis stretched between vehicles for shade from the hot sun. Some enterprising individuals had already taken advantage of the situation, strolling up and down the long line of trucks selling newspapers, paan, chai and pakoras.

The crowd blocking the road was becoming agitated. Most of

them had been drinking, and the sour smell of *handia* (the local beer) hung heavily in the hot still air. We sat sweating in silence as they pressed up against the jeep. The District Forest Officer, who had gone ahead, returned to inform us that nobody was to be allowed near the scene until all the negotiations were finalised.

We waited at a forest office while discussions continued well into the night. Everybody was determined to get their money's worth. The local politicians had now arrived in their blacked-out vehicles, eager not to miss this opportunity to milk a situation, and they pushed their way quickly and arrogantly through the people who had gathered outside.

I worked my way through the mob, squeezing myself into a position from which I could see into the room. The District Forest Officer was sitting behind a large desk which protected him from a group of angry men who were gesticulating, yelling and shaking their fists.

I caught the general drift – much of the conversation was conducted in English,

'*You*,' they shouted vehemently, 'must assure us that *your* elephants will not enter the gardens in future.'

It was extraordinary. It was as if the District Forest Officer owned the elephants and was personally responsible. Then the crowd started demanding permanent employment for labourers, better conditions of work and compensation for the dead woman. In India, the sum due for a person killed by a wild animal is about 7,000 rupees (roughly £150).

The District Forest Officer remained calm. He had handled situations like this before, but I could see the strain written on his face. He quietly promised medical aid to the injured child whose mother had been killed and immediate financial compensation for her bereaved husband.

By this time the heat had become unbearable and I fought my way back through the crowd.

Meanwhile Aditya had been hard at work. 'Read this,' he said, holding out a scrap of paper as he limped towards me. 'I overheard this conversation at the paan shop between the paan-wallah and one of his clients. They were talking in Bengali, so I found a gentleman to translate it for me.'

I read the piece of paper. It was indeed extraordinary.

Paan Wallah	What is happening in range office?
Other Man	Usual bargaining that is taking place after such a killing.
PW	Who all are there?
OM	Everybody – forest people, labourers, manager and the *netas* – the political leaders.
PW	Have you idea what happened?
OM	Why not. I have gone to site and seen for myself. The dead body is lying on the ground, trampled very badly. It is extremely bad sight.
PW	I am not knowing why elephants kill people like this.
OM	I think woman must have abused elephant using bad language. You know how these people are getting drunk during evenings. She must have lost her senses to abuse elephant. You know woman had baby in her arms whom elephant did not cause any harm at all. Elephant could have snatched baby but instead elephant put it aside and only then killed the mother. Naturally abuses of woman was too much for elephant to stomach. But see. Even when elephant had been angry it spared the child – is it not amazing?
PW	Yes indeed. But see fate of child and father.

In India deaths caused by elephants are more often than not considered to be the victims' fault, such is the reverence for this great beast, the symbol of the mighty god Ganesh.

Aditya told me of a similar incident which had taken place further east in Assam. One evening a herd attacked the labourers' living quarters. Everyone ran away, except an old woman and a heavily pregnant younger woman who could not move fast enough. The elephants trumpeted and thundered their way through the settlement. The old woman dragged herself to safety but the pregnant woman was unlucky. A stray elephant crashed through her hut and crushed her to death. In the silence after the animals' departure the old woman heard the clear wail of a human baby. Scared silly, she nevertheless dragged herself towards the cry. At the side of the dead woman lay her newborn baby screaming at the top of his voice. Afterwards the manager of the tea estate adopted the child. Now the foundling attends a college in Calcutta where he is reputed to be a fine sportsman and scholar. People say there is something special about him. His name is Ganesh.

The crowd had now almost dispersed. Negotiations were over. The tension had eased. In fact there was a general air of conviviality which, considering the circumstances, I found unsettling. Hands were shaken, backs were slapped and the fat-cat politicians eased their bulks back into their cars and slid off into the night. Aditya noticed my consternation.

'Strange, isn't it,' he grimaced, 'how the poor get poorer, the rich get richer? It is the story of my country . . . but I think we can help.'

'How?' I demanded.

'Well, obviously we want to film the body . . .'

I agreed reluctantly – it would be dramatic and relevant to the film – but the thought was both disrespectful and distasteful.

'In that case we'll have to pay to see it,' Aditya added.

I was appalled. The situation was bad enough without the indignity of paying to view death.

'You don't understand, Mark. This is India. Let me explain. The government compensation is likely to be about 7,000 rupees. Tragically, for the poor man whose wife has been killed it is a no-win situation. As a Hindu the most important stages in life are birth, marriage and death. These all have to be commemorated by religious ceremonies – the bigger and more lavish, the better. Not to perform these rites is a terrible smear. The poor suffer the most from this system, exploited ruthlessly by the priests. Therefore the family has to borrow money from a middle man to enable them to perform the puja. It sometimes takes three years for compensation to grind its way through the wheels of bureaucracy. Interest accrues, and by the time the money actually arrives, the family is inextricably in debt. So', he concluded, 'by giving him money we are actually helping him.'

I still didn't like it.

'Okay,' he said. 'I'll check with the District Forest Officer and the dead woman's husband. Let them decide.'

He returned a few minutes later. 'The husband has agreed. We need to give a donation of 1,000 rupees.'

Like an entourage of undertakers, we drove off and eventually parked on the main road, walking the three hundred yards from there to the labour lines. It was dark. We stumbled our way along a maze of small paths between tall privet hedges that divided the simple adobe dwellings. The low moaning which filled the air grew louder as we entered the compound. It was like a scene from hell – torches stuck into the trampled earth illuminated a sea of wailing people. Friends and relations were sobbing hysterically, banging their heads in anguish against the ground.

The crowd parted as we walked forward, loaded with camera gear, into this pool of private grief. As we got closer the pleasant smell of incense scarcely camouflaged the sweeter and more pungent smell of death. On the ground lay an old, threadbare blanket. Someone pulled it back. What lay underneath was hardly human. It was difficult to believe that a few hours before this had been a strong and healthy woman. Now, like a small rag-doll which had been pulled and crushed by a petulant child, she lay on her side – if it was her side – her legs splayed at extraordinary angles. Her kneecaps were flattened and a dark curtain of blood-matted hair partly disguised her hideously disfigured face. Looking at this unfortunate creature, barely distinguishable from the mud in which she lay, I could feel clearly the intense rage of the elephant as it had picked her up and slammed her into the ground time and time again. It was as indelibly marked as a stamp.

I walked away and let the unfortunate crew get on with their distasteful business.

The District Forest Officer was standing, his arms around the bereaved husband whose eyes were rolling uncontrollably.

'What has happened has happened and it cannot be undone,' he said. 'We will do whatever is possible to help you.'

The man tore himself away in anger. 'Sir, it is easy for you to say this. But look at my wretched condition. You have lots of elephants. If some are killed, still you will have some left. But my wife will never be back again. She is lost for ever. My little son is in hospital, badly injured. Maybe he will survive. But can you tell me how I can grow him up without his mother? Everything is ended for me.'

The man fell to his knees, sobbing. The District Forest Officer looked at me and shook his head in despair.

'Thrice this has happened in so many days. Maybe three hundred people per annum are killed by elephants in my country and it is getting worse. What can we do? We are understaffed. We do not have manpower or vehicles. Every week I come to these areas and I give a talk. I tell them to cut their hedges so that they can see what is beyond. I tell them not to plant bananas or grow paddy, but then how can they survive? How will they eat? I tell them not to brew alcohol in their house. This is what happened here. The elephant came through there. It smelt the handia.' He pointed to a gap in the hedge and two small holes halfway up the side of the flimsy mud structure of a hut. 'See, he was a tusker. He was beginning to push the house when the woman ran out carrying her child. It was dark, there was no moon. She did not see the elephant – she ran straight into it.'

I asked about the child.

'The child was lucky. The mother must have thrown him away before the elephant grabbed her. His injuries are not too serious.'

The moaning reached a crescendo as the pathetic bundle was unceremoniously carried away and dumped in the back of a jeep.

We returned to the camp. Parbati was sleeping. Aditya and I stoked up the fire and sat drinking in silence. All around us the pitch-battle raged on. Lakhi and Kanchen fidgeted in the gloom. We did not sleep well that night.

8

Back on the Road

The familiar ping of stone hitting metal roused me from a deep but troubled sleep. I looked at my watch. Damn! I had overslept. I struggled out of my tent. Parbati was in full gun-slinger's gear, pouring water on to the ashes of the still smouldering fire. I rubbed my eyes and looked around. Something was different – the camp had disappeared. In the pilkhana, Phandika and Dino sitting on two fully loaded elephants were making final adjustments to the ropes. Parked close by was our back-up vehicle – a battered long-wheel-base jeep – the farmyard transferred to its roof-rack as Poni and Babul fought a losing battle to secure the chickens. Aditya, Poni and Babul would travel in this vehicle, and go on ahead to select suitable campsites. It would be just like the old days on the road with Tara – with one exception. Aditya would not be able to travel by elephant, because of his bad leg. I would miss him.

I breathed a sigh of relief. Judging from the sounds that reverberated noisily from the frog, I was not the only one to have overslept.

'I'm sorry, Parbati. We came home late and . . .'

'It does not matter. You needed sleep. But do not be too long. We must get started before sun is too hot.'

By the time Aditya and I had packed up our things, Parbati and the film producer were bending over the bonnet of the jeep, studying what looked like a piece of paper. I peered over their shoulders. It was an old map, dating from around the middle of

78

the last century. A thin unbroken line of forest, marked on the map by little trees, ran east along the Himalayan foothills. This area is known as the *Duars*, which literally translated means 'passes'.

Parbati pointed to the forested area. 'This is our journey. Always elephants migrate along here. Now, there is little forest. Just tea gardens, villages and towns. I hope you all like tea.'

'Isn't this area the proposed "corridor" that India and Bhutan were going to replant and set aside exclusively for the use of the migratory elephants?' I ventured. I had read about it in the newspapers.

She cut me off contemptuously. 'Corridor!' She spat a thin jet of chewed tobacco. 'What do governments know? They sit in offices making big plans to show they are doing something. But they are not. Corridor cannot work here. Too many people, too little forest. This is worst area for elephant problem in India. But it is good that we are taking this journey. People will then see and learn before it is too late.' She stabbed her finger down in an area on the map showing a swathe of thickly forested tracks further east in Assam, 'Beyond here, it may be possible to do something. *Here* there are good forests and big herds. But now there are different problems. It is dangerous. I do not like to go there.'

The producer and I looked at one another. Originally we had planned to follow this route through West Bengal and end up in the great wildlife park of Manas bordering Bhutan and Assam, where, we had thought, we could film undisturbed elephant habitat.

Parbati caught our look. 'Already terrorists and poachers have killed and even kidnapped foreign people working in this area. Just last week one forest officer was tied with rope and hung. Both his elephants were shot. I cannot risk your lives or lives of my elephants. We will see when we get there how it is. Then I will make decision.'

I lingered over our route. It brought back memories of my other journey with Tara – of how, with the aid of a few similar old maps, we had wandered across her country at our own pace and will. This was going to be something different.

'Hurry up, Mark!' Parbati shouted. She was already mounted on Lakhi, tapping her leg impatiently with her little bamboo stick.

Kanchen bent her head and, grabbing her ears, I swung up easily, stepped on to her head and settled my backside on a gunny bag that Phandika had spread across her shoulders. Gone now was the luxury of the cushion and the howdah when riding Tara: this was the real thing. The hours of square-bashing that I had endured under the eagle eye of Sergeant-Major Phandika had hardened my feet and legs so that I no longer needed the unsightly bandages. I threaded my feet through the stirrups and dug my heels sharply backwards to indicate to Kanchen that I wanted her to reverse. She complied willingly and, executing a perfect three-point turn, lumbered smooth as silk out of the pilkhana behind Parbati. Soon I was being lulled by the soft shuffle of Kanchen's feet and the horror of the previous night became a distant memory. Back on the road. Back on elephants. There was no better way to go.

A sharp digging in my ribs disturbed my day-dreaming. I glanced over my shoulder and saw Phandika's brown eyes glittering.

'Hey, Bandoo [brother] – smoke?'

I pointed anxiously at Parbati who was pushing on at a fair pace in front. Phandika smiled and shook his head. He muttered something to Kanchen and she turned off the road. Like schoolboys, hidden by the thick luxuriance of a bamboo grove, we enjoyed the excitement of a forbidden cigarette.

We quickly caught up with Parbati. Dino had taken over and Parbati was reclining on the gudda behind him. With her head comfortably supported by her arms, she was gazing into the vast blue void above.

'If you must smoke, Mark,' she said, 'carry finished cigarettes with you. Do not leave on ground.'

I turned furiously on Phandika who was leaning over the back of Kanchen and making some intricate and totally unnecessary adjustments to the rope looped under her tail.

'How did you know?'

She turned on her stomach, her eyes impenetrable behind her dark glasses, and smiled, exposing that sharp white pointed fang. 'All my life I have known that old man. After my papa died, he looked after me. He taught me much. But now I am his boss, and it is difficult for him. He is older than me and I have to show him respect. But if *I* want respect, I have to be clever. Like all mahouts, he is cunning. So I must be more cunning. Bring Kanchen alongside. I will tell story. Then perhaps you understand.'

I urged Kanchen forward. Immediately the two elephants greeted one another by entwining their trunks, and trundled along, side by side, like a pair of fat old teapots.

Parbati pointed to a small cloth bag that was tied to the gudda just behind me. 'Oranges. For you – I put them there this morning. Give me one. I am thirsty.'

She skinned it with a tiny curved kukri and cut it into four segments which she distributed among us.

'There is belief in my part of India,' she said, spitting out a pip, 'that foxes are the most clever of all animals. It is believed that lawyers, who are very clever people, are born from parents who have eaten seven foxes; from parents who have eaten fourteen foxheads mahout comes out; but from parents who have eaten twenty-eight foxes comes cleverest of all – elephant owner. Now,' she concluded triumphantly, 'you understand how I keep that old fox under control.'

*

It was getting very hot. The sun slammed down on to the surface of the tarmac road that stretched into the far distance before us, turning it into a black molten river. There was no shade. We stopped regularly to allow the elephants to slake their thirst in little stagnant pools.

From the slow build-up of trucks that swerved past us dangerously, I guessed that we were approaching the outskirts of a town. Parbati grimaced and covered her face with her gumcha, shielding herself from the toxic fumes that were enveloping us in clouds.

'We go left here,' she said. 'I do not like towns.'

We cut across country – if one could call it that. Apart from a few tired clumps of bamboo and the odd graceful grove of betel nut palms there was hardly a tree in sight. But there were villages, and with the villages came people – thousands of them, as they swarmed like an army of ants – hoeing, cutting and reaping every inch of this cultivated soil.

Judging by the hostile looks we received as Lakhi and Kanchen picked their way delicately like tight-rope walkers along the high narrow ridges that separated the fields, these people were not pleased to see us, but as I glanced at the high wooden *machans* that stood like fortresses guarding each allotment, I understood why. For them, living as they do with the reality of wild animals as neighbours, elephants meant destruction.

Occasionally people would come out from their houses and pay obeisance to the great god Ganesh, who for Hindus is ironically the deity that represents protection, with gifts of oranges and stalks of sugar cane. But as India's population increases by twenty million each year, the reverence that has surrounded this gentle creature for centuries is being inexorably eroded as people and animals fight a duel to the death for survival.

The American naturalist, Charles Frederick Holder, wrote prophetically more than a hundred years ago:

> The Asiatic elephant is said to be holding its own. But the rapid advance of the British in the east cannot fail to have a fatal effect and their extermination is only a matter of time. They are the last of a powerful race worthy of earnest efforts for its preservation. The question of its extinction rests with the rising generation.

As we drew nearer the distant hills we were afforded a glimpse of forest, stretched out in a ragged line, like a depleted army making its last stand against the vast squadrons of tea gardens, which glittered like emeralds in the afternoon sun. Into this strange and sterile environment we rode. It was to become our home for the next few weeks, for the owner of one of the largest tea corporations in the world had generously put the facilities of all his tea gardens at our disposal.

The film crew had already established camp on the tea estate's football ground when we arrived. The place appeared to be in uproar. Was this merely a reflection of the huge and fanatical following enjoyed by Indian cinema, I wondered, or something more sinister? I looked in puzzlement at Parbati as we threaded our way through a tunnel of riotous colour as the tea labourers lined the road in throngs. She shrugged. I could sense her discomfort. She hated crowds.

'What the hell's going on?' I asked Aditya as we arrived at our camp at the other end of the field. Parbati interrupted curtly.

'Go and wash elephants,' she said.

Wearily I went into my tent and changed into my lungi. It was clear that being a film star did not absolve me from my duties.

'Wait, Mark,' Parbati called. I clambered back outside to find her staring intently at the bright blue sky, her nostrils twitching. 'It will not be necessary. Rain is coming.'

'Nonsense,' I said, surveying the idyllic conditions, and turned to join Phandika and Dino.

A mischievous smile flitted across her face. 'Nonsense, eh? We will bet. If rains, you buy me new sunglasses. Mine are no good. If no rain, you do not clean pilkhana tomorrow.'

'Done,' I replied, holding out my hand to seal the bet as she whacked hers down on mine in a traditional black greeting.

Aditya and I wandered across the football field to check out the crew's camp. On the way we were intercepted by a smartly dressed young man wearing a blue Lacoste T-shirt, black shorts, long white socks and multi-coloured trainers. He was followed by a bunch of some of the roughest individuals I had ever set eyes on. They were carrying a terrifying assortment of medieval weapons – machetes, a kind of homemade pistol, and a bow and quiver full of arrows with wickedly barbed tips.

The smartly dressed man held out his hand. 'I am the assistant manager. Welcome. Unfortunately, the manager could not greet you himself. He is busy in the factory. But he has asked me to pass on his good wishes and to let you know that you are welcome to use the facilities of his house any time you wish.'

We thanked him and he gestured to the villains.

'These are your security. They will patrol the area at night. One cannot be too careful.' Shaking our hands again, he took his leave.

Aditya studied our security, who by now were wandering off peering into the crew's tents in curiosity, leaving a strong smell of local hooch in their wake.

'Biharis,' he stated. 'They'll be so drunk tonight they'll need security.'

A chill wind suddenly got up, and I saw a grey mass of cloud, not unlike a herd of moving elephants, approaching from the east.

'Sunglasses and dung-clearing,' Aditya said. 'You'll never learn. In future let me negotiate.'

We hurried back to the camp. A few fat spots of rain were already staining the canvas. Parbati was lying curled in the entrance to her tent, looking like a small, dangerous and smug cat.

'Okay, you win,' I said, retreating into my tent as heavy rain started to fall.

'The bet is off, Mark,' she shouted, raising her voice above the downpour.

'No, I'm a gentleman,' I replied gallantly. 'A bet's a bet.'

'If you insist. But for me it is easy to tell these things. I learn in my papa's university. The university of nature. You cannot survive in forest without this knowledge. But now, my knowledge is maybe useless. There are no universities any more.'

The camp was suddenly illuminated by a flash of lightning, and there followed a heavy rumble of thunder.

'Rain,' she continued, 'comes because they cut forest. Nature is turned topsy-turvy. It will bring problems. Wild elephants will come from hills. It is too slippery there. They come into these gardens. It is dangerous time. But, at least Lakhi and Kanchen are happy.'

She gestured towards the pilkhana where, hardly distinguishable from the black mire of their vast mud bath, the two elephants were submerged like two fat old ladies at a health spa, rolling around in ecstasy.

'Well,' I said, peering through the cascade of falling water, 'it's cold rations for us tonight.'

Parbati looked perplexed. 'Why? Dino is cooking.' She pointed towards the mahouts' quarters where Dino was squatting over a blazing fire and stirring a pot with one hand while holding a banana leaf over his head with the other. 'We always carry dry wood.'

After a sumptuous dinner of rice, potatoes and spicy little grilled fish, we sat comfortably in the entrances of our tents. The rain had now stopped – or so I thought.

'Eight litres. Lakhi,' Parbati said without looking round. She was right. I peered rather rudely around the tent, to find Lakhi, her legs splayed, noisily relieving herself.

*

It was dark and still raining when Parbati woke me.

'Wake Aditya and get dressed quickly. I have received message. Forest elephant has been injured by wild tusker. I must treat her.'

I noticed that she was carrying the little cardboard box filled with glass bottles which I had seen in her tent. A jeep was waiting outside, and we set off into the driving rain.

On a forest road we found the wounded elephant being pushed along quickly by her mahout, who was sheltering under an umbrella. He looked agitated. The tusker, we discovered, had attempted to mate with her during the night. In the ensuing struggle, as she fended off his amorous advances, he had stabbed her left front leg with the point of his tusk.

Elephant owners in this part of India prefer, and even encourage, their domestic females to mate with roving bulls. They believe the offspring will inherit the natural vigour and strength of their wild fathers. There is a saying that whilst you can take an elephant out of the jungle, you cannot take the jungle out of an elephant.

Here, however, was a clear case of attempted rape. The poor creature stood suffering her pain quietly, hardly flinching as Parbati gently probed the deep wound. I could not understand why her mahout did not wait with her at the compound until help arrived, thereby sparing the elephant the additional pain of this long walk. Parbati explained as she quickly mixed the contents of her medicine cabinet in a small bowl. The mahout, it seemed, was doing the only sensible thing. Earlier the tusker had tried again, but the mahout had managed to drive him away with fire-crackers. Just then a terrible shrill trumpet pierced the air, followed by a crashing of trees.

'See,' Parbati said nonchalantly, 'he is coming once more.'

Aditya and I looked at one another and then eyed the jeep, both of us realising that this metal box would be no match for four tons or more of angry elephant. We cast worried looks down the jungle path, while Parbati cleaned the gaping wound and sang to calm the injured elephant. She interspersed her singing with a lengthy diatribe on the pros and cons of modern and traditional medicine, which, I'm afraid to say, fell on somewhat deaf ears. At last she finished. I breathed a sigh of relief. She told the mahout to take the elephant slowly back to the forest headquarters.

Our driver climbed into the jeep and turned the ignition. Nothing happened. At the same moment there was the sound of a tree being contemptuously flung aside, and a few hundred yards further down the road a large elephant appeared. The driver leapt out, flung open the bonnet, fiddled around with the engine, got back in and tried again. Nothing happened. By now the tusker – closer and bigger – was strolling towards us with all the arrogance of an urban street punk. Suddenly he extended his ears and trunk. He had seen or rather sensed us and broke into a rambling half-trot, half-walk. Aditya and I both dived into the jeep to join the driver. At least it offered some protection. The last thing I heard was a bellow of rage followed by the sound of crashing branches. Nervously I lifted my head and peered through the windscreen. Parbati was standing in front of the jeep.

'Mock charge. Elephant only means business when trunk is tucked in mouth. Trunk is elephant's most prized possession. He will not risk it.' She laughed. 'Men – such cowards.'

Our driver eventually got the jeep started and we caught up with the wounded female, already moving more easily.

'See,' Parbati said happily, 'she is already better. But she must have injection when she gets home, to stop infection.'

The elephant gently extended her trunk and caressed Parbati's long black hair. I noticed the elephant's eyes were wet.

'She's crying,' I said.

'Wouldn't you?' Parbati added softly.

9

The Magnificent Mal Squad

Exhausted by our nerve-racking encounter and our disturbed sleep, Aditya and I decided to take advantage of the manager's kind hospitality. A hot bath, we felt, would restore our equilibrium. Parbati, who I now realised was a natural adrenaline junkie, was keyed up by the early morning drama and in a remarkably good mood. She excused me my duties for the rest of the day. We set off through the tea gardens. The weather had now cleared and, but for the tea pluckers who seemed to float mysteriously like brightly-coloured buoys on an emerald sea, Aditya and I could have been enjoying a stroll on a golf course on a sunny day in suburban Surrey.

The tea pluckers, I noticed, were mostly female. In Asia, Aditya told me, picking tea is women's work, due to their greater patience, dexterity and soft hands. I also noticed that they were making strange hissing sounds as they moved in an orderly and colourful line through the bushes.

'Snakes,' Aditya said. 'Snakebites are a common occurrence in the tea gardens. Particularly in the wet season. That's how they drive them away.'

Here and there among the tea bushes umbrella-shaped trees, their canopies stretching gracefully outwards, stood like guards on a green parade ground.

'Those are the all-important shade trees,' Aditya explained. 'They protect the valuable bushes from burning up in the hot sun and provide some shelter to the tea pluckers.'

We watched the women squat down to rest and quench their thirst from the urns carried by the water wallahs. I now understood the derivation of the word tea-break. Even the children were looked after. A familiar wailing emanated from large green caravans with mesh sides, parked on the side of the roads. I peered inside one to be greeted by a hundred little dark faces cosily encased in little hammocks that stretched like cobwebs across the interior. A group of elderly women squatted nearby, too old now to endure the back-breaking work of plucking. Their job was to reassure and comfort their grandchildren in these mobile nurseries while their mothers worked in the gardens.

'You know you're seeing the very best here,' Aditya remarked as we wandered past a neat row of adobe huts. 'These are the labour lines.' He pointed to a thick electric cable supported on iron poles. 'They even have electricity. But this is not the case in many gardens, such as the one where the woman was killed. The conditions there are very different. They are real sweatshops – maximum output, minimum input.'

Through a freshly painted, white five-bar gate a gravel drive, edged by neatly trimmed rose-beds, led grandly to the portico of an imposing colonial house. Beyond the flower beds a sweeping lawn ran up to a thick and luxuriant bamboo hedge, draped in crimson with the flowers that had fallen from the flame-of-the-forest trees that grew behind. Against a child's swing a gardener was sprawled, taking a nap. The hum of bees filled the air, and in the distance the familiar drone of a lawn-mower evoked memories of long hot summer days in a very different part of the world. I yawned, overcome by the peace and serenity of these surroundings. To a visitor like myself, the quiet life of a tea planter up country did not seem to have changed a great deal from colonial days. But, as I was to discover later, appearances could be deceptive. Today's managers have inherited a dilemma – and as night falls they are waging what amounts to a war.

I experienced another evocation of England when Aditya and I climbed the broad stone steps leading on to the veranda of the house – the tantalising smell of frying bacon. The manager's wife, a handsome and immaculately coiffeured woman dressed in a beige silk shirt and matching tailored cotton trousers, welcomed us. We followed her across the polished marble and into a large, cool hall at the end of which a solid mahogany staircase ascended to the next floor. Tasteful arrangements of flowers stood in thick crystal vases on the occasional tables, creating vivid bursts of colour. Somewhat out of place, an old-fashioned ice-axe with a worn wooden handle hung on one of the high white walls. The manager's wife noticed my interest.

'The ice-axe belonged to Sherpa Tensing,' she said proudly. 'He gave it to my husband, who was a great friend.' She laughed. 'We cannot claim it reached the top of Everest but it did accompany him to 28,000 feet. Now, let me show you to the guest room. I hope you'll find everything you need.'

It was an understatement. It would have been a treat even if we had not spent a couple of weeks under canvas in an elephant camp. She ushered us into a suite of rooms of which any five-star hotel would have been proud. 'If you need anything, please ring that bell.' She wafted away in a cloud of scent.

In the bedroom were two large beds their covers turned down revealing crisp, freshly laundered white sheets. There was even a mini-bar – full of bottles of chilled water, various soft drinks and a solitary bottle of ice-cold beer.

Aditya looked at his watch. It was ten past eight. 'What the hell,' he muttered as he popped the lid and sprawled on the sofa in front of the television. I went to explore further. In the bathroom there were three different kinds of shampoo, conditioner, sachets of bubble-bath, shower caps, large fluffy towels and plenty of hot water.

An hour later we emerged smelling like roses, to find a full breakfast laid out on a large wooden table in the dining-room. Ravenous, we attacked a mountain of sausages, bacon, baked beans, chips, fried bread and four different egg dishes. This was followed by thick slices of toast spread with creamy butter, marmalade and local honey. But the best was yet to come. It was all washed down with pots of steaming hot, freshly brewed coffee.

Later the general manager arrived, a strong, fit, bespectacled

man of Nepalese origin, wearing what I assumed was the costume of the modern-day planter – half-pants, short-sleeve shirt,
socks and trainers. We settled down on comfortable chairs on the
veranda and enjoyed their premier brew served in fine white china
cups.

He explained that on this tea estate alone, and it was by
no means the largest, he currently employed one thousand
eight hundred people. And this number doubled during the
busy season. I began to understand the scale of this industry –
tea was big business.

I asked about the elephant problem.

He sighed. 'Just here, and in my neighbouring gardens, we've
already lost sixteen lives this year. But we do everything we can
to protect our people. Apart from electricity, I have my own special squads who patrol the gardens and labour lines at night with
tractors and searchlights. Still the elephants come in. They damage the shade trees, the tea bushes and unfortunately the labour
lines.'

He spread out a selection of photographs on the table. I picked
one up. It resembled the aftermath of a nuclear holocaust.

'Where else can they go?' I said. 'These areas were once all
forest.'

'It was the English', he replied, 'who started this industry
well over a hundred and fifty years ago. But it is only in the
last twenty-five years that the problem has escalated.'

I took his point. By the year 1900 over a million acres of
inaccessible jungle had been cleared by the British in north-east
India and in Ceylon. Harnessed by man, elephants had helped to
dig their own graves. In those early pioneering days, they represented the only safe means of transport in these wild and remote
areas, quite apart from their traditional role of timber extraction.

'I suppose, Mr Shand,' he continued, 'if I were sitting in Delhi
and read in the newspapers about the extinction of the elephant, I
would react differently. Unfortunately that is not the case. Here I
have three thousand six hundred people to protect and they come
first.'

India's modern-day planters have been presented with an

unenviable legacy. In the old days there were plenty of elephants and plenty of forests: conservation was not an issue. Nowadays these green, manicured oases provide some shelter for the wild migrating herds but the cost, in human terms, is high. As the manager emphasised, while the planting of tea has certainly not helped the plight of the Asian elephant, it is not in fact the main cause of the problem. The real problem is the human population explosion.

The manager pointed to the pretty bamboo hedge. 'Elephants come into my garden every night. There was one particularly cheeky fellow, a big tusker. My wife and I watched him every evening from here. He would wander in, scratch himself leisurely on the swing, trample over my wife's roses and take a drink from the swimming-pool. He was shot the other day in another tea garden by a member of one of the government elephant squads. Now,' he added, 'if you really want to see some action go out with those boys.'

*

Somewhat cautiously, I broached the idea to Parbati of spending a few days with one of the elephant squads. I mentioned that I was worried about shirking my duties as a chaarkatiya and neglecting Kanchen. Parbati reassured me.

'It is important you see these things. You must understand. Do not worry about Kanchen. Elephants never forget. And do not worry about me. As you see this morning I have many things to do.'

*

Every area has its own government elephant squad whose sole job is to protect the villages, farms and tea estates from raiding herds, and it was with one of these squads that we were to spend the next few days. The Magnificent Mal Squad was led by the legendary Captain Bhattacharjee, a man whose heroic actions have taken on almost folkloric proportions. He had been known to walk calmly up to a rampaging wild tusker and give it such a severe telling off that it turned tail and fled in terror.

In some trepidation we entered the run-down building in down-town Mal Bazar which served as the headquarters of the government of West Bengal's range officer's wildlife squad. It was empty and quiet but for the irregular ticking of a clock. Massive, heavily padlocked cabinets lined one wall. On another wall hung a large and detailed map. Centre stage was held by a battered wooden desk covered in stained green leather, bare except for an antiquated black telephone. Overhead a fan turned lazily.

'Anyone home?' Aditya shouted. There was silence. He shouted again.

From somewhere in the back of the building we heard the sound of voices. One was raised in anger, then we heard a scuffle and a crash, as if something heavy had fallen on the floor. At that moment a young man arrived looking harassed. Aditya asked if we could see the captain. He shook his head and mumbled something incoherent.

'The captain is apparently in full bed rest,' Aditya explained. 'We will come back later.'

At that moment a half-naked figure, wearing only a long woolly balaclava and a lungi that he was struggling to hold up, lurched wildly into the room. If it had not been for the helper's timely and, I realised, well-practised intervention, there might have been a nasty accident as the new arrival tripped on one of his undone bootlaces and flailed uncontrollably towards the desk. The young man steered him gently into the old battered chair behind the desk. The newcomer then broke into paroxysms of violent coughing, his face turning pale and his eyeballs spinning alarmingly. He fumbled in his lungi, pulled out a crumpled pack of bidis, lit one with a shaking hand and wheezily inhaled. As the smoke exploded from his nose and mouth his face regained colour and his eyes steadied. He leant backwards in his chair and waved his arm in the air in what I imagined was some kind of salute.

With that he disappeared, to grope around beneath the desk, cursing. He reappeared and placed a bottle of brandy reverently on the desktop. A decorative label depicting a small Indian man sporting an immense handlebar moustache, and the national costume of France – striped T-shirt and black beret – advertised the contents of the bottle: 'Honeybee brandy – made from the choicest grapes from India and France. A little bit of France in every sip.' We christened this ingenuous and lovable character Captain Honeybee. To this particular brandy he showed the same unbending loyalty and devotion with which, we soon realised, he treated his men – he would never waver. Honeybee, and only Honeybee brandy was good enough for him.

'Vine,' he said thickly. 'You like vine?'

I checked my watch. Although it was still only eight-thirty in the morning I knew that it would be quite impossible to refuse.

As I took my first sip of Honeybee, which, despite the extravagant claims of its advertising, bore no relation whatsoever to its supposed country of origin, I tried to work out what it was about the captain that was so appealing. He possessed few teeth, his face, when not ashen, was an unhealthy yellow, his watery old button brown eyes and hanging jowls gave the impression of a mournful bassett hound, and yet there was something quite irresistible about him. I was tempted to reach over, pinch those pudgy cheeks, pick him up, pop him into my suitcase and take him home.

Our companionable drinking silence was abruptly broken by the urgent ringing of the telephone. Honeybee leant slowly forward, picked up the receiver and laid it on the desk. He then topped up our beakers with brandy. The disembodied voice of a woman could be heard squeaking from the receiver – hello, hello . . . hello, hello – swiftly followed by the click of disconnection. Honeybee replaced the receiver. It rang again, and he did exactly the same thing. This was a common occurrence, as we were to find out later from his helper, and showed another side to this delightful character – cunning.

Usually his staff answered all calls. He only spoke on the telephone when absolutely necessary – and there was a reason for this. Honeybee feared nothing and no one except for his wife – a high-born Brahmin, who was most disapproving of his liquor consumption. He never drank at home. Depending on his condition, he would call her back later that day or the next, armed with a variety of excuses. His favourite was: 'My dear, I do apologise. You caught me at the most unfortunate moment. I was eating and my mouth was full of rice . . .'

With some difficulty, Aditya managed to extract permission from the captain for us to accompany the squad that night. Then the sound of badly changed gears and the wailing of a siren on the road outside announced the return of the previous night's squad.

'Squad coming, squad coming,' the captain croaked. The door crashed open and a bunch of bearded men, heavily clad in green balaclavas, mufflers, and old-fashioned military greatcoats and carrying an assortment of rusty old shot-guns, batteries, searchlights and other paraphernalia, burst into the room. They smiled cheerfully and shook our hands, making no comment as the helper dragged the ailing captain from his desk into another room. Aditya was soon deep in conversation with Honeybee's second-in-command, whose fierce looks belied a gentle and almost scholarly nature as he explained the never-ending problems they faced.

'Every single night of the year,' he said, 'we are on permanent alert. There are eighteen members of the squad, which is divided into two shifts – one night on, one night off. But when you are off duty you cannot sleep.'

'Why do you do it?' I asked. 'Surely you could find a more restful job.'

He smiled, gesturing to the back room, from which a deafening snore could now be heard. 'Because of him. He is a good man. We trust him. We respect him. He protects us. He is our father. If we have family problems he will listen and give us advice. We never go short of food. If we have no money he will give it. If we have problems in our work he will stand up for us. We are his family and we will willingly lay down our lives for him.'

Such devotion in government circles in India, let alone the rest of the world, is rare, but already I could understand why. I asked him about the tusker that the squad had shot recently.

'Ah,' he said. 'You have heard about that. Master Shooter, as we have christened him, is not here. But, it was not quite as you imagine.' He picked up one of the rusty old shot-guns. 'These are all we have to defend ourselves and we do not like to use them. Instead we use the rockets and bombs.' He pointed to a pile of gaudy boxes stacked in the corner of a large cupboard that stood open. 'This time it was different. We had to save a man's life. The goonda had broken a labourer's home and picked up an old man. It was fortunate that we were close by. Master Shooter ran up to the elephant. He had never fired a gun before. He pointed it in the air and fired to scare the elephant. It was amazing. The elephant dropped down dead, just like that. He had misaimed and hit the elephant right between the eyes. It was sad. But one man was saved.'

I lifted the cover off one of the boxes to inspect their ammunition more closely. Considering that the box held rockets, the gaudy label was slightly misleading. It depicted a pretty young Chinese girl wearing a little coloured frock and white socks. The packaging on the next box I opened was more appropriate – two elephants standing on their hindlegs, their entwined trunks holding an exploding golden star. But the contents – curiously named 'chocolate bombs', enticing little balls wrapped in glittery paper – looked more like Christmas decorations.

I wandered outside to inspect the squad's vehicle. Another bearded man was furiously rubbing a long deep gouge in the side of the driver's door.

He looked up. 'Tusker, sir, last week.'

As I looked inside my eye caught the sparkle of the decoration that bedecked the interior of the cab. In the centre, smiling benevolently, hung a small familiar effigy, half-man, half-elephant, the god of protection – Ganesh.

The Magnificent Mal Squad chariot was a four-wheel-drive truck painted pale green and powered by a diesel Mahindra Jeep engine. The driver and radio-operator, who fielded the messages from the base station here at Mal Bazar, were encased in relative safety in the hard-top cab. The back was simply covered in canvas. Inside, two long wooden benches stretched down either side and on the top between the cab and the canvas a special wooden plank had been fitted for spotlights. It looked an unwieldy and under-powered machine for such operations.

Aditya had organised everything. We were to report back at four thirty sharp. To kill time until then, we decided to see what the town of Mal Bazar had to offer.

10

A More Dangerous Animal

A large sign, which read 'S. Mukerji and Sons, Purveyors of Fine Indian-Made Foreign Liquors', hung grandly over a dismal one-storey building whose front was protected by a row of solid bars. A few locals were squeezed up against this steel cage, staring longingly at the delights on display in the dark and dingy interior.

'Window shoppers,' Aditya announced dismissively. Sweeping them aside, he banged firmly on the bars. A small wizened man looked up from behind a massive pile of ledgers. 'He doubles as a money-lender,' Aditya whispered, clearly an authority on such establishments. 'These guys make a fortune.'

Mr Mukerji's eyes lit up in the gloom. Here are potential big spenders, he clearly thought as he approached the front of the shop.

'Two bottles of Director's Special,' Aditya demanded.

Mr Mukerji scuttled off into the dark confines of the shop and soon returned with the merchandise. He handed the bottles through the bars to Aditya.

'Four hundred rupees, please sir.'

'And the four glasses,' said Aditya.

'What glasses, sir?' the man replied.

'The two complimentary glasses that you are giving away with each bottle of Director's Special.' Aditya pointed to the display poster.

'Oh sir, that is very old. No glasses now.'

'No glasses, no whisky, no money,' Aditya retorted firmly.

There was a tense silence. A crowd had now gathered. Mr Mukerji's eyes narrowed, weighing the odds – both whisky and money were on the other side of the bars. His business sense prevailed and, muttering crossly, he scuttled to the back of the shop again, returning with four glasses engraved with a jolly logo.

'Money?' he demanded.

'Glasses,' said Aditya.

Reluctantly Mr Mukerji passed them through the bars and Aditya handed over the money. The crowd was delighted and fell about laughing. Clearly it was not often that someone got the better of Mr Mukerji.

Our next port of call was Kedar's Stores. Apart from owning the Harrods of Mal Bazar, Mr Kedar was not unlike an upmarket paan-wallah. Obviously this was *the* place to meet, judging by the number of smartly dressed tea planters' wives who gathered in perfumed groups, enjoying a giggle and a gossip. Mr Kedar's store seemed to sell everything. Like an over-stuffed pillow, bursting at the seams, it exploded out on to the pavement in a riot of colour and bizarre bric-à-brac. Hanging on hooks from the awnings were cricket bags, feather dusters, American ankle socks, VIP special Frenchie briefs (India's sexiest brand of men's underpants) and, oddly, a beach set complete with parasol and large inflatable ball.

I wandered inside, my nostrils tantalised by the heady, evocative and pungent smells of spices. On high precarious shelves an amazing assortment of tinned food jostled for space. There were many western delicacies on display; I now knew where my breakfast had come from.

The treasure-trove seemed inexhaustible. Barbie dolls, bathroom scales, condoms in three different colours, thermos flasks and curiously erotic candlesticks. Under glass-topped display cabinets gold jewellery glittered seductively. For those long after tiffin evenings on the tea estates there were also games – Scrabble, Scruples, Monopoly and dominoes.

I looked around in wonder. 'You have everything, Mr Kedar.

And rats!' I shrieked, as a particularly large and scaly-tailed rodent ambled across my bare foot.

'Of course sir,' he answered logically, 'if one is selling the very finest of goods one is having rats.'

In the end I settled for two pairs of white gym shoes for Phandika and Dino. Phandika had been complaining recently that he did not own any shoes. To honour my bet with the boss, I bought a sinister pair of wraparound sunglasses. I thought she would look splendid in them.

Armed with our goodies, we arrived back at Mal Bazar headquarters in good time. There was still no sign of the captain, but the squad was there waiting, drinking tea, filing reports, replenishing explosive supplies and cleaning shot-guns. Everybody seemed relaxed but underneath I sensed an air of expectancy. At precisely six-thirty the black antique telephone rang. The second-in-command picked it up, listened intently and then replaced the receiver.

'*Chalo!*' – or in other words, 'Scramble!'

Just like those brave pilots who waited, nervous and impatient, day after day, night after night, during the Battle of Britain, the Mal Squad, mufflers flying, dashed out into the night, followed closely by Aditya and myself. We jumped into the waiting truck, its engine already running. Siren wailing, the driver threaded his way through the congested back lanes of Mal Bazar and, once clear of the town, began climbing steadily. I stuck my head out of the window. It was a clear and bitterly cold night. A full moon illuminated the empty road in front of us. Turning off the main road, we entered a tea garden and approached a small white bungalow where an agitated man was waiting. Without a word he pulled open the cab door and squeezed in beside me. Following his urgent instructions, the driver thundered along the maze of little avenues that criss-crossed the tea gardens. The spotlights were turned on and a blaze of light flooded across this eerie and silent oasis. Piles of steaming dung littered the tracks, dropped by the panicked elephants as they fled somewhere just ahead of us. The driver threw the truck round a righthand bend, almost tipping it over, and there, just ahead of us in the spotlights, filling the windscreen, was the hurriedly retreating backside of a female elephant in full flight, its tail extended rigidly in panic.

As we swung round the next corner the rest of the herd came sharply into view – twenty of them in all shapes and sizes, including a dozen small calves, squealing in terror as they crashed through the tea bushes.

I felt desperately sad. It was the first time I had seen these majestic and beautiful animals reduced to the level of common and rather cumbersome thieves. Stripped first of their forests and now of their dignity, they ran like frightened rabbits in the headlights of the truck.

The driver slammed on the brakes and the squad bailed out of the back, carrying an assortment of rockets and bombs. They rushed through the tea bushes and I quickly followed. For the next few minutes I was treated to a dazzling and deafening pyrotechnic display as the squad stood their ground in a thin ragged line and resolutely drove the elephants down an escarpment. We heard them reach the bottom as they crashed over the stones of a dry river bed.

It was then that nature bared its awesome teeth, humbling us all and the fireworks display with its brilliance, as a great blue comet arced gracefully across the sky. It lasted so long and was so bright that we were afforded a clear view of the retreating elephants far below, illuminating briefly a flash of pure white at the front and the back of the herd. They had now been joined by two tuskers. This was a rare sight. For in a perfect environment the herd is led by the matriarch and only visited by males during courtship. Now, as they are driven from one tea estate to another, from one village to the next in their desperate search for food, the added protection is necessary. They simply have nowhere to go.

On that and many other nights, we raced from one tea garden to the next, following much the same pattern. Sometimes, due to the expertise of the squad, we were able to cut off the elephants before they even entered the tea gardens. 'They know we're coming', they told us proudly. I believed them.

The trouble while filming was that the Mal Squad truck lacked manoeuvrability and acceleration. The general confusion was also causing the cameraman problems. To ensure good, clean, dramatic shots he said we needed to get closer to the elephants. I gulped. They seemed quite close enough to me. All the same, I respected his opinion. He was highly experienced, with many films to his credit, and he had also filmed elephants before – although perhaps in a less stressful environment.

The tour operator, whose vehicles we were hiring for the film, was dismayed when we commandeered his personal automobile – a brand new blue soft-top Suzuki jeep, with nice blue velour seats to match – for the exercise. The soft top was soon removed, and so were the nice blue velour seats. Into the back piled the cameraman, strapped in tight by a special harness that provided some stability and enough freedom to manoeuvre his heavy hand-held camera, the sound man with all his equipment, the cameraman's assistant with a mobile generator to power the spotlight, and the producer. I was in the driving seat. Riding shotgun beside me – armed with one of those rusty muskets and a few boxes of chocolate bombs – was a member of the Mal Squad. I was connected to Aditya in the Mal Squad back-up vehicle by means of a two-way walkie-talkie.

It was a hair-raising business, racing along the narrow bumpy tracks between the tea bushes in the pitch black. For the sake of the camera, we wanted to get as close as possible without announcing our approach in a blinding beam of light. At the same time I had to measure my distance and avoid ramming a fleeing backside, towering above the bonnet, or provoke these spooked out titans into making a swift turn and charging straight towards us. There was neither time nor space in which to turn the vehicle round and get the hell out. When the cameraman judged the moment right, the generator would be fired up, on would go the spotlight and, whatever happened, the camera would begin to roll.

There were other obstacles to contend with too. On many occasions I had to hit the brakes hard to avoid running into the numerous large limbs that had been ripped from the trees and were blocking our path.

'Those bloody elephants are doing this on purpose,' I grumbled as I sat behind the wheel watching three of the film crew struggle to lift a heavy branch out of the way. The cameraman ribbed me good-naturedly about my mad theory of elephants deploying classic military tactics.

'You're just tired, Mark,' he said.

I was tired – but not mad. Elephants are no ordinary creatures. In these areas at the beginning of the century, wild elephants had shown their displeasure at the intrusion of new railroads that were being constructed by continually pulling down the telegraph-poles lining the tracks. In the end, engineers had to fix the wires to trees.

One night we devised our own military tactic – a kind of pincer movement – to outwit the elephants. We now knew the exact movements of a particular herd. After leaving the tea gardens they would always traverse a large meadow, crossing a narrow track at the same place on their way back to the forest. Our plan was for the Mal Squad to drive the elephants towards us while we waited a few hundred yards down the track. As the herd neared the crossing point Aditya would alert us by means of the walkie-talkie and we would then race into action.

We waited quietly in the darkness. It was a cold and moonless night. Beside me sat our security, smoking a bidi, his fingers playing with the safety catch of his musket. Click, click. Click, click. In front of him on the dashboard lay a row of chocolate bombs, primed and ready to go.

Soon, in the distance, we heard the hullabaloo begin. Rockets took off. Chocolate bombs exploded in dull thuds. The walkie-talkie squawked.

'Get ready,' Aditya's voice crackled.

I started the engine. The cameraman's assistant fired up the generator. I lit up a cigarette. The walkie-talkie squawked again, this time loudly.

'Go, go!' Aditya yelled. 'The herd is crossing further up.'

I let out the clutch and promptly stalled the engine. The jeep lurched and stopped.

'For Christ's sake, Mark!' the cameraman yelled.

'Sorry.'

I fumbled with the ignition and the vehicle shot off in a cloud of dust. We raced along the track. In the distance the spotlight just illuminated a mass of moving grey, like a passing cloud.

'Faster!'

I floored the accelerator. But it was too late. The herd had already crossed and were running rapidly into the forest on our right. I slammed on the brakes.

'Dammit! I couldn't . . .'

'Don't worry,' the cameraman interrupted wearily. 'We'll get them another time.'

We moved off slowly. Suddenly the walkie-talkie squawked again.

'Stop right there!' Aditya's voice crackled urgently. 'You've cut off a calf. It's on your left.'

The cameraman's assistant swivelled the spotlight and we could just make out a small shape at the bottom of the meadow.

I picked up the walkie-talkie. 'It's too far to film, Aditya. We're on our way . . .'

'Do not, I repeat, *do not* move. There's a tusker on your right. He's coming back for the calf. You can't see him. He's behind that hillock on your right.'

'Get ready, John,' I said, picking up speed.

'You idiot!' Aditya yelled. 'The boys have told me he'll go for you. Reverse right now!'

Frantically I fumbled with the gearstick. The squad member had now realised the danger. He stood up on the seat, lit a chocolate bomb with his bidi and hurled it on to the track ahead of us.

The explosion was muffled by a terrible shrill trumpet of rage, numbing all our senses as a huge shadow threw us into darkness. The jeep shook violently, as if in the vacuum left by a passing express train, as the tusker thundered across the track in front of us and crashed away into the night.

For a moment there was silence, followed by a long exhalation of breath from the back of the jeep.

'Well,' the cameraman said, 'that was a close run thing.'

I gripped the steering-wheel hard to stop my hands shaking. Far too close, I thought, as I remembered the deep gouge in the side of the large and solid Mal truck.

★

One evening, as a change from chasing elephants, Aditya and I visited the local tea planters' club. I suppose because of its name, I had conjured up images of long cane chairs, the click of billiard balls on green baize, and the clink of glasses as burra-sahibs in tweeds and flannel trousers drank chotapegs of whisky from thick crystal tumblers. I was to be disappointed. This was not colonial but modern India.

We were greeted by a barrage of flashing red lights and the deafening blast of Seventies disco music as 'Saturday Night Fever' reverberated around an empty dance floor. At the bar a crowd of noisy young men dressed in bell-bottomed polyester suits, and matching ties and handkerchiefs, drank Bullet beer straight from the bottle. The beer was aptly named for, as it struck its target, the more exaggerated the elephant stories became.

We escaped into the garden. Quietly enjoying the cold night air was a splendid old Indian gentleman dressed more traditionally in a nice fluffy cardigan, corduroy trousers and a neat paisley cravat. Mr Sen, it transpired, was one of the oldest planters in north-east India. He had begun his apprenticeship some forty-nine years ago under the British. Curiously he did not see much change in the tea industry except, he added wryly, the colour of the skin. He missed the camaraderie and community spirit of the club-house of those bygone days. 'Nowadays,' he told us sadly, 'we only meet once or twice a month. They all stay at home and watch those bloody fillums.'

A couple of nights later, while out once more with the Mal Squad, I witnessed another situation which the squad regularly faces, and it involved a much more dangerous animal – man. A herd of elephants had entered the labour lines and it was said that someone had been killed. This, as we found out, was not true but merely a rumour that had been fuelled by vivid imagination and the local hooch. When we arrived, a drunken crowd, brandishing torches, surrounded the truck, yelling that the squad had come too late and demanding immediate payment for the bereaved. The men filed out and tried to calm the situation down. A knife flashed in the torchlight and a rock bounced off the shoulder of one of the squad members in front of me. A mob in India is always dangerous, but a drunken mob is lethal. We quickly got back into the truck. The vehicle lurched alarmingly as they surged towards us and tried to tip it over. The boys in the back let off a few rockets which momentarily parted the crowd. The driver seized his chance and we accelerated away in a barrage of rocks.

The radio operator conveyed the news of this over the transmitter to headquarters, and when we returned to Mal Bazar a very different Captain Honeybee was there to greet us. He was stone cold sober, and from the insults that he was hurling over the telephone to the manager of the tea estate, he was obviously livid.

'How dare you treat my men like this, you son-of-a-pig. I'll come over right now and beat the hell out of you with my shoe. I'll kill you.' He then slammed down the receiver, picked it up again and dialled another number. It was to his boss, demanding immediate legal action.

By now the squad had become like brothers to us, and we were very touched when they asked us to become honorary members. On our last day we decided to take the captain out for a farewell lunch. When we arrived he appeared in familiar mufti, sarong and woolly balaclava, unusually alert and clearly agitated.

'He's here,' he hissed, 'he's here.'

I looked at Aditya, perplexed. Who on earth was 'he'?

He turned out to be she, in the shape of a large handsome woman draped in an elegant sari who gazed disapprovingly down on all three of us. 'He' was his wife.

We invited her to join us. She declined, saying that as it was Sunday she had many things to do. The captain soon reappeared this time dressed in shirt, trousers and a windcheater, the balaclava perched on his head and his familiar old boots with the laces flapping loose.

'I will not be taking obnoxious things,' he whispered mournfully to us as we climbed into the jeep, 'he is here, he will know.'

'Absolutely Captain,' Aditya acknowledged, 'not a drop.'

As we neared the hotel the captain leaned over anxiously, 'Well, maybe just a little obnoxious thing.'

We feasted on fish curry and rice and a little obnoxious thing – a bottle of Honeybee. While we ate, he told us a story about Laljee Barua, Parbati's father.

'Oh Baba,' he said, 'Laljee was not a man. He is taking five bottles at a time. Open, drink and throw, open drink and throw. He was a god.'

After lunch, I was just paying the bill when there was a tremendous crash from outside. I rushed out to find the captain in a dishevelled heap at the bottom of the stairs, being helped to his feet by Aditya. Miraculously, he was unhurt, and in fact it had sobered him up a little, which, considering the predicament he was facing, was not a bad thing. How, he moaned, was he going to explain his condition to his wife? But the captain, it seemed, was a past-master of these situations.

'You must tell him,' he jabbered incoherently, 'that I did not want to take obnoxious things but because we are brothers, and sad at parting, you forced it upon me. I did not want to take it.'

I could not believe that this was going to wash, but I readily agreed. When we arrived back at headquarters, the captain hovered behind us. Aditya explained the situation to his wife, telling her that we had forced a drink, but only one, upon him to celebrate our friendship and imminent departure. Clearly she did not believe us and glowered disapprovingly at the captain who had another flash of inspiration. 'Take fillum of us all,' he shouted at Aditya.

This suggestion appealed to his wife's vanity and Mrs Honeybee insisted that first she should tidy herself up. The captain was delighted. Whether this new plan would put her in a good mood or not was hard to tell. She soon returned, freshly coiffed, and Aditya recorded this strange trio for posterity.

We made our farewells. As we climbed into the jeep a happy Honeybee lurched out.

'Today saved,' he said, 'today saved,' and with that odd salute, he disappeared again back inside.

I hoped he was saved. We would never forget him.

11
Elephant's Graveyard

It was a relief to be riding elephants again, rather than chasing them. Over the next few weeks we headed slowly east. The landscape varied little – just one tea garden after another, punctuated by strange little pockets of forest. It was not long before I began to resent the monotony of this artificial terrain. As early as 1911 the *Eastern Bengal District Gazetteer* recorded:

> Few districts in India have developed as rapidly as the Western Duars. The northern tract along the base of the hills is now covered by prosperous tea gardens. Little jungle is left, except on the banks of the rivers and the streams and cultivation is spreading fast.

Aditya went on ahead in the jeep to search out campsites, but generally we ended up as guests in the tea gardens. A nice cup of tea had begun to take on a different meaning. I was not the only one to be affected. In one garden we spoke to the manager's wife who had spent her whole life in this area and had never drunk a single cup of tea. Not that I was complaining – the generosity was overwhelming, but I began to feel like a tourist on a guided tour of country estates rather than on some great journey by elephant.

Parbati felt the same way. Her moods, which had previously been a little unpredictable, now became constant. In the forest she came alive, bubbling with enthusiasm as she happily pointed out different flowers, shrubs and trees. In the tea gardens, hunched between Lakhi's great ears and driving her on at a cracking pace, she grew silent, almost menacing. Wearing the dark wraparound sunglasses – now an almost permanent fixture – she looked the ultimate Easy Rider.

Phandika, on the other hand, was in his element. Although in the Indian caste system mahouts rank fairly low, their macho job controlling such huge and awe-inspiring beasts makes them irresistible to the female sex. They are the sailors of the elephant world – tough, proud, roving Casanovas, with a popsy in every pilkhana – and tea gardens provide rich pickings.

By the end of the day, my ribs would be black and blue as, with the aid of his bamboo stick, Phandika drew my attention to the shapely and colourful delights undulating beneath us in the tea bushes. 'Right side, sir' . . . 'left side, sir' . . . and then with a suggestive nudge he would illustrate his intention with that all too familiar gesture which he somewhat curiously described as 'pik-pik'.

It seemed from what he told me, as he acknowledged the admiring and shy gaze of a particularly beautiful young woman by gallantly taking off his woollen bonnet, he also enjoyed the perfect marriage. You go and enjoy your life, his wife had told him. All I need is a set of clothing and a square meal. The world is yours, not mine.

Beauty pageant aside, these days also provided the ultimate test for an amateur physiognomist like myself. No other area in India possesses such a bewildering mix of people. This is partly due to its geographical position, a narrow corridor which connects it to the rest of India, bordered by Nepal, Bhutan, Sikkim and Bangladesh. But it is also due to the tea industry. In the Thirties, the city of Ranchi in Bihar was one of the great recruiting centres for coolie labour, and the results, now into their third generation, are clearly stamped on the faces of these people. Transmigration and intermarriage have mixed the squat, dark features of the Mundas and Santhal tribals with the paler and more mongoloid features of the mountain tribes.

During these long rides my training continued, from both Parbati who continually made me practise my commands, and from Phandika who, when he was not jabbing me in the ribs to check-out a chick, jabbed me between the shoulder-blades to keep my back straight. Parbati also imposed a strict riding routine – one hour on, one hour off. I was not sure whether this was enforced to ensure a quicker pace, or a thoughtful gesture to ease my aching legs. Either way, it gave me a wonderful opportunity, as I spread myself comfortably on the gudda, to study the extraordinary bond between these elephants. Many times I saw Kanchen snatch a passing branch, break it into two, drop it on the road and leave it for Lakhi to enjoy. This little gesture only confirmed my thoughts about Tara – she definitely needed a pal.

The joy of travelling with two elephants is that you have ample opportunity to observe the other. I frequently watched Lakhi plodding behind me, that long and curious proboscis missing nothing. She had a strange penchant for plastic bags, which she would pick up and wave around like little flags.

In the towns and villages we were mobbed by hordes of screaming children. For a moment, it brought back happy memories of villages in rural Orissa – until they started throwing stones at the elephants. I shook my fist and shouted to them to stop, but Parbati simply ignored them and reassured me.

'Baini, Baini. These are children. They know no better. They see elephant. They see death.'

Fortunately these barrages did not last long; movie posters soon diverted their attentions. Dogs were a different matter. Parbati hated them. These snarling scrawny curs descended in packs behind the elephants which would abruptly stop, whirl round, and bellow in rage. Parbati brought out her deadly catapult and the dogs were picked off one by one to slink away squealing in pain.

'Bloody things,' she said angrily, fitting another stone into her sling and letting fly, 'are one reason people are killed by elephants. When elephants try to pass through villages at night dogs come out and bark. Elephants get angry and follow dog back home. Then they destroy house and people inside. If I was prime minister, I would have them all eliminated. What good do they do? Nothing.'

I agreed with her. Well, at least in India. I had often had to beat a hasty retreat in the tourist spots from these wretched and ravenous scavengers. It may well have been the British who were to blame for the dog blight. According to Lockwood Kipling, it is not impossible that these were descendants of the mastiffs which Sir Thomas Rowe presented to the great Mogul Emperor Jahangir in the sixteenth century. Such was their viciousness that one of them was said to have jumped overboard on the voyage to India and attacked a school of porpoises. On their way up-country, another savaged a full grown elephant, grabbing it by the trunk. Unfortunately the emperor was very taken by these sweet little things and provided them with servants and carriages in which to take the air, and he had silver dishes and tongs made in order that he might feed them with his own royal hands.

Leaving the towns behind, we traversed dried-up, pebble-strewn riverbeds, not unlike the beaches of the coastal resorts of south-east England. Once raging torrents, they now lay dead and lifeless, blocked up and silted with the deposits of the dolomite mines that pitted the hills above us like angry white scars. As we pushed through little patches of forest I gained some idea of what this whole area must once have been like. And 'pushed' is the right word; Parbati, perhaps for her own peace of mind, always chose the most impenetrable routes.

I spent some uncomfortable moments avoiding an avalanche of ants and spiders as Phandika, wielding his kukri with the ease of a master swordsman, cut a passage through the thick and luxuriant foliage. It was the stillness of these little plots of paradise that struck me most. Apart from the incessant whirr of cicadas, high in the fern-covered trees overhead, and the occasional sharp rat-a-tat-tat of a woodpecker attacking a tree stump, it was so quiet that one was almost startled by a falling leaf.

Somewhere, I imagined, hidden deep in what was left of their homes were the elephants, sharing these quiet moments, perhaps sleeping, perhaps bathing or perhaps playing with their children. I now understood why Parbati had chosen this route. Like all great teachers, she had simply shown me the way, allowing me to draw my own conclusions.

It was growing colder now, and in the mornings a light dusting of snow lay on the violet foothills that rose gently in the distance. Aditya and I took to waiting for the sun to rise before performing our morning ablutions. These began with us loudly invoking the name of the great Lord Shiva to give us strength and courage. O Bholay, O mighty Bholay, O Bholay Shankar!

This new battle cry stemmed from a meeting with a strange sadhu that Aditya had found presiding over a roadside shrine to Lord Shiva, one of the most powerful of Hindu deities. Aditya was not a religious man. Perhaps seduced by one of Lord Shiva's multi-faceted personalities relaxing on a tiger skin in his heavenly Tibetan palace at Mount Kailash, surrounded by his weird and wonderful cronies, Aditya had decided that we needed further personal protection for our journey and he was 'our man'.

We bowed reverently in front of the garlanded shrine. The saffron-robed sadhu anointed our foreheads with crimson, then in a cloud of perfumed smoke gently rested his hands on our heads. Closing his eyes the holy man began to chant and chant and chant . . . It seemed as if it would never end.

'What was he saying?' I asked Aditya afterwards, stretching my back, numbed both mentally and physically by the power of the sadhu's mantra.

'Search me – probably a recipe.'

'A recipe!'

'Well, he told me earlier that he's only just renounced the world. Last week he was employed as a cook on a tea estate.'

India – you could not beat it. Blessed by a chef – what next?

Either the chef or the great God Shiva had indeed bestowed blessings on us all. A few days later at a rural village we received a very different welcome. A group of elderly men and women appeared from one of the large huts that surrounded their neat compound to make their obeisance to Lakhi and Kanchen. They were short and stocky, with darkish yellow skin, and jet-black straight hair framing high-cheekboned oriental features. One old woman was puffing contentedly on a small silver pipe.

'Rhaba tribals,' Parbati said. 'They worship elephant.'

The women were dazzlingly attired in iridescent cholis, blood-red lungis and large cummerbunds, glittering with threads of woven gold, and they wore spectacular jewellery – silver-beaded necklaces hung like chokers of pearls around their necks, matching the solid heavy bangles that encircled their wrists. In their noses were small delicate studs, fashioned like lotus flowers.

Rhabas are animists, and they are especially fond of both celebrations and alcohol. But they like to drink in secret, brewing their *chakat*, as it is known, in large pots and then transferring the alcohol into hollow bamboo containers. Aditya – never one to miss the opportunity to sample the immense variety of elixirs that his country has to offer – managed to organise a private tasting and we sneaked off seemingly unnoticed. In the dark confines of one of the huts we finished off three bamboo pipes.

It was not long before we rejoined the main group – definitely in a party mood. When I climbed back on to Kanchen, only a slight twitching of nostrils below those dark glasses indicated that Parbati had guessed the reason for our absence. Phandika was furious and jabbed me hard in the ribs, indignant that we had not included him.

A discordant clanging of cymbals and beating of drums announced the arrival of the band. There was also a strange bellowing sound not unlike a cow in labour, which emanated from a long bamboo tube which a gentleman was blowing furiously. For the next two hours, from our lofty elephantine perches – like honoured guests in a private box at the opera – we were treated to a bizarre and spontaneous display of celebration. The dance followed a circular movement as the band, followed by the women, shuffled, clapped, sang and gyrated in ever-increasing circles. As the afternoon wore on and the chakat had its effect the dancers seemed to join as one in a riotous blaze of colour – like a hungry flame – as they whirled faster and faster below us.

It was getting late. Parbati indicated that we should move on. We padded away, unnoticed by the Rhabas. Later, in the distance, we could still hear them celebrating.

We camped that night in the shadow of a plantation of tall graceful betel palms which, illuminated by the glow of the fire, seemed to soar up behind us, perfect in their symmetry like the pipes of an organ. Exhausted by the day's celebrations, I turned in early, but I could not sleep. I crawled out of my tent to find Parbati gazing into the fire and occasionally turning the glowing embers with a small stick.

'Something bad will happen,' she said without looking up. 'I can see it in this fire. Fire is my friend. It tells me things. Sometimes it laughs and it is happy. But now it is laughing in different way. It is angry. It needs feeding.'

I shivered.

'It is difficult for me, Mark,' she continued. 'I am educated person. I attended school but that school taught me nothing. This school', she said, pointing to the fire, the sky and the trees, 'taught me everything. It has never let me down. My friends and family, they think I am mad. Just silly superstition, they say. You are modern woman, not jungle woman. You must paint your toenails and all silly things like that. But each time I do, something bad happens. It is like I am two people in two different worlds. For man, even today this life is okay. But for woman, it is difficult.'

After she had left, I sat for a long time by the dying fire, thinking about what she had said. Parbati was a victim of her upbringing – a child raised in the forest who now found herself an adult woman in a very different world. She was, I realised, not unlike her elephants, born in the wild and now captured by her environment. But unlike the elephants which perhaps longed to go back and could not, she had a choice which was, in a way, so very much more difficult.

*

The next morning a forest jeep arrived at the camp to take Parbati to tend a sick female elephant that had collapsed on the outskirts of a village. We piled into the jeep and raced off. I noticed that Parbati was tense, very tense, and from the whiteness of her knuckles as she gripped the seat I could also see that she was very angry. I wondered why. I would have thought that in her line of work she would have become somewhat hardened to this increasing occurrence, but from her behaviour today I sensed that there must be something else – something more personal.

Again it was as if she had read my mind. 'I know this elephant,' she said quietly, her voice choked with emotion. 'For months I have tracked her with her family. I see she is very sick. She is thin. Her head is shrunken. Now she has left family. But they would not have abandoned her. She would have made decision and told her family to go on.'

'You mean,' I asked, 'that she is a loner, a *female* loner?'

Even I, with my limited knowledge of wild elephants, knew that this was quite unheard of – males, yes; females never. Elephants have often been seen, particularly in Africa, refusing to leave a massacred corpse. They have remained at the scene, bewildered and defiant, even trying to lift the dead elephant to its feet.

'Yes,' Parbati said, banging her fist on the dashboard. 'You see what is happening now. This is first time I have ever seen it. And I have been watching elephants all my life . . . Oh God, I hope we are in time.'

We had left the road and were taking a bumpy and twisting track that snaked its way through the paddy fields towards the hills. They were almost bare, except for a few pockets of green which stood defiantly like the last tufts of hair on the pate of a balding man.

We travelled on in silence. Parbati's shoulders suddenly shuddered. She turned to me. 'It is too late. She is gone.'

To our left, in a small paddy field, a crowd had gathered. Parbati leapt out of the car and ran towards them. Aditya and I followed slowly with the rest of the film crew.

The elephant lay stretched on her side like some giant and ancient boulder that has been ravaged and pitted by time. Her legs were outstretched. They had gouged great scars in the earth where she had struggled bravely, but hopelessly, to get back on her feet. Her trunk was extended, the tip curled tightly round a tuft of grass in a last minute attempt to gain strength. Her tail had been bitten off – no doubt the result of a fracas with her sister in the wild and now a strange and poignant reminder of happier times. Someone had closed her eyes and paid their respects. A small posy of marigolds had been laid on the elephant's head.

Parbati recovered her composure but her grief was replaced by cold rage. 'See,' she said, pointing to the little pockets of raised skin that peppered the dead elephant's neck, shoulders and flanks.

I ran my hand over the skin. I could feel little hard lumps. 'Pellets,' Parbati said, 'from guns – she is full of them.' She pierced the skin with her fingernail. It erupted in a spurt of stinking yellow pus. From the crater she extracted a sharp fragment of lead. 'From this they get infection and will die slowly, horribly. So many elephants around here are like this.'

She studied the piece of lead in her hand and then angrily flung it away. 'It is not only problem. She is starving. There is disease. We will wait for vet to perform post-mortem. I think it is from cattle. We are seeing many such cases.'

The vet and his assistants soon arrived to perform the autopsy. I did not envy their task. Under his supervision and with the aid of a few simple and crude tools – an axe and a few sharp knives – they swarmed over the body like an army of hungry ants, hacking, chopping and ripping.

Parbati could not watch and sat at a distance under a tree. I remained for a while, morbidly transfixed by the awful carnage. I had seen many animals gutted but this was different. Perhaps it was the sheer size of the carcass that was so dreadful. I knew the vet and his team were only doing their job, but I found it distasteful and undignified. I felt she didn't deserve this. The flies and the smell got the better of me and I went to join Parbati, pushing my way through the large crowd that had gathered, covering their noses and spitting. They stood, as I had, mesmerised by the bloodbath which lay in front of them.

Parbati was sitting quietly and I squatted down beside her.

'I hate smell of death. My papa used to say that elephant smell is better than all perfume of Paris.' She shook her head. 'When will it stop? How can we make it stop?'

The vet called us over, his ghoulish work finished. The results – the heart, liver, and kidneys – were neatly displayed on a

Abandoned by the wild herds, young calves adjust uneasily to captivity

A tiny baby arrives at the orphanage

Playing games in the bath

Little beasts of burden begin training at an early age

A strange encounter with the five-legged sacred cow

Parbati and Phandika demonstrate the art of lassoing

River crossings

That long
proboscis misses
nothing

Lunch in a forest camp

Carrying the forest away

Mark and Parbati at Matiabagh Palace, Parbati's ancestral home in Assam. *Inset:* Laljee Barua, Parbati's father, out hunting on his beloved elephant Pratap Singh

A welcome rest … for some

Celebrating the harvest festival, *Magh Bihu*, with Parbati's sister, the great folk singer, Pratima Pandey

banana leaf as if in a butcher's front window.

'I have taken blood samples too,' he said, 'and will send these off for analysis.'

It seemed that Parbati was right. Bullet wounds were not the only cause of death. The vet produced another piece of the elephant which resembled a large pink sponge.

'This is tongue,' he explained. 'It is thrice its normal size and heavily ulcerated. She would not be able to take food. I have seen this before. We think it is spread by cattle which graze illegally in these areas. They must be stopped. Soon, we will be having epidemic. Many more elephants will die.'

The vet picked up his macabre parcels and departed.

A large pit had now been dug and filled with lime to deter scavengers. They had already arrived. The vultures sat patiently and silently in a large tree. Below them in the dust were their competitors – a pack of scrawny dogs – growling, salivating and fighting among themselves, driven almost mad by the feast in front of them.

Ropes had been tied around the legs of the elephant and we waited for the arrival of a forestry elephant to drag the corpse into the pit. I looked around me. It was, in a strange way, a fitting place for her to rest. It was a graveyard, a graveyard of trees. Little grey stumps like tombstones marked the place where other giants had crashed to the ground and rotted, a silent and forbidding symbol of man's destruction.

The elephant arrived, a tall and magnificent tusker. Quickly the ropes were attached. On a command from his mahout he surged forward, massive shoulders bunched and taut, as he strained to finish his distasteful task. He failed three times, and then, gathering his last reserves, surged forward once more and, as if his great heart had been broken, he emitted one long, terrible shrill trumpet and pulled his sister into her grave.

As we prepared to leave, Parbati told us to go back to camp without her. She would join us when she could. She had more work to do. The remains of another elephant had been found in a forest nearby, this time the victim of yet another kind of threat that faced these animals. Poachers.

It was late by the time we got back to camp. The boys were sleeping and Aditya, his face drawn with exhaustion and pain from the long day and bumpy drive, soon joined them. But I could not sleep. There had been so much death and still I carried it with me, its pungent odour clinging to my clothes. It was on my hands, in my hair and in my beard.

I took a towel and walked down to the little river and immersed myself, oblivious of the cold. Gradually the icy waters exorcised the horrors of the day.

Needing company and reassurance, I went and joined Lakhi and Kanchen who were chained beneath a tree. For a long time I stared at them as they rumbled happily to one another between mouthfuls of fresh fodder. Like Tara, I thought, they may not be free. But as the terrible images of the day came tumbling back into my mind, I thought at least they are alive.

12

The Creeping Sore of Totopara

Aditya was fed up with the jeep. He wanted to be back on the road, on an elephant. Fortuitously, Parbati had sent word that her work was not yet finished and Phandika was to press on without her. A spare seat, so to speak, had become available.

We were heading for Totopara, a remote village situated on the Bhutanese border and the last bastion of the Totos – a tiny tribal community of which only thirty-six families exist today. Phandika, it seemed, was not enthusiastic about our destination. Apart from being dangerous country, infested by desperados that stalked the lonely roads, the women, he maintained, were *very ugly*. There was no alcohol and the people were full of disease. The last time he went there, he told us, he had itched for days.

'Just my luck,' Aditya grumbled as Dino effortlessly picked him up and deposited him on the back of Lakhi. 'But the old fox is probably exaggerating.'

'Not according to Mr Amal Kumar Das's book on the Totos,' I replied, thumbing through my notebooks and finding the relevant page. 'The road to Totopara is dangerous,' I read. 'Monstrous leeches and pythons add to the terror and lie in wait . . . The Totos believe their women [once] had very good looks. The people of Bhutan, and Mech and Garro, tried to entice away their women and in fact carried some of them away. They appealed to their god Mahakal and he gave the women bad ulcers and made them ugly and thus saved the women.'

After a short pause I continued: 'He goes on to discuss their personal hygiene. He says the Totos are very dirty and rarely wash. After eating they do not wash their mouths. They use stones and leaves after evacuation, not water. The Totos think that if they wash frequently they will catch colds and die . . . They are carrion eaters – cattle mauled by tigers or even diseased are eaten with great relish. Apparently they also suffer from a special kind of creeping sore which is deadly – known as Toto sore.'

'What a charming place,' Aditya remarked. 'But at least Mr Das does not tell us that they abstain from alcohol. We're bound to find some good hooch there and, if not,' he added patting his bag, 'we have Mr Mukerji's best – a couple of bottles of Director's Special.'

'What about Parbati?' I asked.

'Parbati, my friend, is not here.'

We set off – it was a beautiful day and we climbed steadily through thick forest alive with birdsong.

'Today,' Aditya announced, looking rather like a startled owl from the magnification of the round grey glasses perched on the end of his nose, 'I am taking over as your guru. Welcome to my country Mr Shand. You will be seeing many wondrous and strange tings.'

We did. He identified – as they flashed across the depth of green like winged gems – little groups of scarlet minivets, and interpreted a strange metallic plaintive sound high above us in the treetops as the cry of the pied-crested cuckoo. I was impressed but also suspicious. The Maratha was blessed with a vivid and playful imagination. He had once amazed a group of serious birdwatchers who were staying at Kipling Camp by recording thirteen previously undiscovered species in one morning. My suspicions I thought were not unfounded when he identified a large group of birds with rose pink and black plumage that were chattering noisily in a tree.

'Pasta!' he exclaimed excitedly, 'lots of pasta.'

This was going too far. 'Sure,' I replied, 'any particular brand, vermicelli, fusilli, spaghetti . . .'

'Not pasta you fool – *Pastor*.'

Phandika and Dino were watching all this with a certain

amount of detached amusement, but they were not to be outdone by the Maratha's ornithological knowledge. We entered a clearing in the forest which was curiously flat and devoid of any vegetation – not unlike the hard beaten surfaces of the cricket pitches in this country. This, they both announced emphatically, was an elephants' ballroom – a *nautch-khana*. Whether fact or fiction, it did not matter as the image it conjured up was too wonderful to disbelieve. According to John Lockwood Kipling in his book, *Beast and Man in India*:

> Let us believe then, until some dismal authority forbids us, that the elephant 'beau monde' meets by the bright Indian moonlight in the ballrooms they clear in the depths of the forest and dance mammoth quadrilles and reels to the sighing of the wind through the trees.

The forest began to peter out and, due to the presence of the *haathi machans* that frequently dotted the banks of the dried-up river beds, it seemed we were nearing civilisation. Phandika explained that the elephant herds migrated here in the summer months to escape the heat and flies of the Indian plains and to enjoy the abundant bamboo forests and salt-licks that lay in the steep virgin forests of Bhutan just ahead.

Parbati's father, he told us nostalgically, had close links with the royal family of Bhutan, and it was in these areas that they had caught some of the finest elephants for the king of this ancient Buddhist kingdom. He even added proudly that it was he who had been chosen to ride the magnificent tusker that Laljee presented to the king in honour of his accession at the coronation parade.

It seemed that ornithology was not the only subject that my replacement guru was going to dazzle me with that day. It looked as if I was in for a history lesson as Aditya fumbled around in the pile of books that littered Lakhi's back, like a strange and ancient mobile library.

He picked one up. From Michel Peissel's *Lords and Lamas* he read: 'The great hill warriors of the Land of the Dragon would descend to rape the women, steal the harvest and exact levies. They always went unpunished as no one dared enter their mountain stronghold.

Even the infuriated British never dared to enter those hills although countless British subjects were kidnapped.'

'Nonsense,' I argued, 'I don't believe it. We must have destroyed them – just like we did the Marathas.'

'Well, my friend, listen to this,' he droned: 'The exasperated English sent an official to settle the problem, the Honourable Sir Ashley Eden, Envoy Plenipotentiary of Her Majesty Queen Victoria. The Bhutanese ridiculed this feathered dandy, obliging him to sign a humiliating treaty, and, in fact, so maltreated him that Sir Ashley Eden had to escape from Bhutan by night to save his life. The treaty was repudiated on the grounds that it had been signed under duress. The Crown had been humiliated, a preposterous, unthinkable occurrence the like of which was to be found nowhere in the Annals of British colonial affairs.'

'Go on,' I said.

'Are you sure – it gets worse,' Aditya said happily, settling his glasses back on his nose. 'For once someone called the British bluff. The Bhutanese let the infuriated British protest go unanswered. They simply captured two mountain guns and defeated a British detachment.'

'And what did the British do?'

'Nothing. It says here that – The following year the same viceroy approved a treaty . . . whereby in consideration of the Government of Bhutan have expressed regret for its past misconduct . . . The British were to give 50,000 rupees annually to Bhutan in compensation for the Duars which the British now annexed. The Bhutanese returned the two guns. The joke was still on the British because Bhutan had never owned the Duars in the first place. Bhutan simply closed its borders to the British and kept them closed whilst collecting its annual revenue. In 1910 the first hereditary king of Bhutan . . . got the annual compensation increased to 100,000 rupees.' Aditya snapped the book shut with a satisfied thud and started laughing.

'Read on,' I said. I knew this story.

'It's not really necessary. Nothing happened.'

'Read on, Aditya.'

Reluctantly he re-opened the book. 'In 1949, after Indian

Independence a treaty of friendship was signed between the Government of India and the Government of Bhutan by which the Bhutanese obtained the return of one of the Duars (which had never belonged to them) and a fivefold increase of this old 100,000 rent. Neither the British nor the Indians were a match for the Bhutanese . . . In 1962 the rent was further increased to one million rupees.'

'You're probably still paying,' I remarked. It was my turn to laugh.

'Lifer!' Aditya roared.

I hit the deck hard, and so did Phandika, who slammed into my back with such force I nearly broke my nose on Kanchen's hard head. Both of us were convinced that we were under attack from bandits. Wincing with pain, I pushed myself upright to find Aditya bouncing up and down like a schoolboy on Lakhi's broad back. Dino thought he had gone completely bonkers and was doing his best to stop him falling off the elephant.

'Lifer! Lifer!' he yelled pointing to a large tree in which a congregation of bright blue birds, glittering like sapphires, were arguing noisily. 'Fairy bluebirds . . . fairy bluebirds. They're lifers for me – never seen them before,' he shouted, quickly grabbing his camera. In seconds he had shot off an entire roll.

What next, I thought, rubbing my nose gently to check for broken bones. This area was dangerous enough without the added histrionics of my part-time guru, and I made a silent prayer for Parbati's swift return.

Fortunately there were no further excitements that day. We were not waylaid by bandits or crushed in the coils of a giant python, and we soon reached Totopara, which nestled cosily in the shadow of a high hill, surrounded by groves of banana trees. Peace, I thought as I wearily dismounted from Kanchen. Unfortunately it was not to last.

★

In looks the Totos were similar to the Rhabas, typical Indo-Mongoloid stock except for a more swarthy complexion due, perhaps, to the high altitude. Although their origins are obscure, they believe that they came from the ancient land of Koch, or Cooch Behar, where they were employed as ammunition carriers during its war in 1875 with Bhutan. Toto, in their language, means ammunition.

In the past there used to be considerable settlements all over the Western Duars but in the last hundred years their numbers have become depleted and the few survivors have settled here in this isolated spot. Totos will never intermarry, and now only about nine hundred of this unique society exist. As animists they worship the forests, the mountains and the elements. Their livelihood depends on the produce of the forests, and as modern India hurtles into the twenty-first century the survival of these tribal people, like that of the elephant, hangs by a delicate thread.

Both Phandika and Mr Das, I felt, had been a little harsh in their criticism of the women. They were not pretty, but neither were they ugly. However a more accurate account of lack of hygiene had been given, for a particularly pungent and unpleasant smell hung over the entire village. I realised it emanated from the innumerable pigs that were kept in pens between the wooden stilts that supported the houses. It was then that I solved the case of the creeping sore of Totopara – without, I may add, any help from the *Merck Medical Manual*, every hypochondriac's essential travelling companion.

The boys had arrived sometime before and the headman of the village had insisted they set up camp next to his house. As head honcho he had the biggest house but also the biggest pigs. Aditya and I had just settled down to sample the delights of India's premier whisky when I felt a strange itching sensation creeping up my legs. It rapidly turned into one of agonised burning.

'Jesus Christ!' I yelled. 'Something's . . .'

'Aaarrgh!' roared Aditya, who was hopping around, banging his hands against the flapping bottoms of his Kurta pyjamas.

Curses of another kind soon filled the air as Phandika, Dino, Poni, Babul and the driver performed similar antics. Only the headman and his cronies remained untouched and, by the looks on their faces, totally amazed by this curious display of devil-dancing.

I fetched a torch. My legs were bright red and covered in black flies.

Suddenly it all made sense. If there were pigs, then there was dirt, and if there was dirt, there were flies – thousands of them. After an icy plunge into the mountain stream that ran below the village we moved the camp to a more suitable site.

*

Like the straw that was beginning to burst from the frayed edges of the guddas with the wear and tear of the journey, we were all beginning to feel the strain. Whether it was due to Parbati's absence, exhaustion, or just too much good old liquor, it was hard to tell, but things got out of hand that night. It started peacefully enough. The itching had subsided, we had dined well, and were sprawled comfortably around the fire, drinking. Phandika had even admonished us with his own set of rules, advising us to drink quietly and avoid conversation.

It was Phandika, however, who soon broke his own rules as the drink began to flow. He told us of his life. His father had died when he was ten and Laljee, Parbati's father, had taken him under his wing. He began as a chaarkatiya on a salary of two rupees a month, but Laljee soon recognised his exceptional abilities and, after just a few years, made him a mahout.

Laljee was a god, he told us, his eyes softening. He had taught him everything. No man could ever have a larger heart. No one could compare with him. He had never seen a man who loved elephants as Laljee did – and they loved him back. He had magic. But it was hard, he continued, in those days. Gesturing towards Poni and Babul, he announced that the boys had it too easy. In the old days being a mahout meant something. There was respect.

There was one elephant, he continued, that Laljee loved more than anything in the world. His name was Pratap Singh. As he mentioned the name he closed his eyes as if in awe. There will never be another elephant like him, Phandika told us. He described how, when Laljee went away, he always left a piece of clothing behind and, if he forgot, then Pratap would not eat. As long as Laljee was around, this elephant would do anything. He could even be ridden in full *musth*. Such was Laljee's love that when Pratap died, Laljee went mad. He stabbed himself in grief. He refused to eat. His family came from all over to comfort him, but such was his sorrow that he never really recovered. He told Phandika and the other mahouts that the work with elephants would continue, but his heart was no longer in it. He carried too much grief. Phandika added that only God would understand so great a love.

The drink by now had begun to take its toll, particularly on the young boys whose tongues had been loosened and were not used to such quantity. Aditya topped up the mugs with the second bottle of India's finest whisky. They began to snipe good naturedly at Phandika, ridiculing his stories, telling him to shut up and calling him an old elephant.

I watched him cuff them affectionately, and order them to curb their tongues. For in a way that is what he was – an old elephant in the last stages of his supremacy, now being challenged by the younger bulls. But he stood his ground. Phandika had been trained in a harder school and there was no way he was going to give in yet.

After Pratap died, Phandika left Gauripur for a while and went to work with elephants in Nagaland, a state further east, on the borders of Burma. A wistful smile creased his battered old face. There, he told us, the women had power. It was a place of magic and they weaved a spell on him. They kept him, fed him, and when he decided to go home he found he could not move. But, he added with a sly grin, he did not want to.

Taking a gulp from his mug, as if needing courage, he told us of a time when he could not escape from the clutches of a woman.

'Oh Baba,' he moaned and shuddered, his face ashen.

It took Aditya and me some time to extract this story from Phandika, such was the terror of the memory. He had been sent by the Indian government, because of his expertise, to teach the Malaysians how to train and handle their elephants. He was billeted in a remote jungle camp. Working in the area was an English woman engaged in primate research. One monsoon there was a flood and they were cut off from the rest of civilisation. The English woman had, according to him, captured him like one of her monkeys, kept him locked up in her hut and used him at her will.

He was a brave man, he told us; he had faced many dangers. He had captured hundreds of elephants, he had controlled hundreds of elephants, he had ridden *thousands* of elephants, but he had never ridden anything like this. She would not stop, he continued. He became thin. Only when the floods subsided could he make his escape.

We all collapsed laughing.

The old fox was mortified. Gruffly he told the boys to fetch some wood.

Poni slurred something and made an obscene gesture. In one quick movement Phandika leapt up, pulled Poni to his feet and whacked him hard.

'Punk!' he spat angrily. Holding Poni by the scruff of the neck, he lambasted us about how little respect they showed. In his lifetime he had seen forty mahouts killed in front of him. Nothing on earth could bump him off, but these boys were killing him with their words. He flung Poni to the ground.

Aditya and I got up quickly to intervene but Dino stopped us.

'No ploblom, sah,' he mumbled drunkenly and, helping Poni to his feet, they all fell into their tent.

Unfortunately there were further plobloms. Aditya and I had barely crawled into our tents before a terrible kerfuffle disturbed us. We shot back out to find Dino struggling to restrain an axe-wielding Phandika who was making wild swings at Poni and Babul. The two boys, scarcely able to stand, were retaliating feebly with their kukris. Intervening, we relieved them of their weapons and ordered them back into their tent. Peace was at last restored as they all passed out.

We recovered all the other dangerous items we could find and carried them back to our tents. By our own stupidity, in encouraging them to drink such strong alcohol, we had created a potentially dangerous situation. It could not be allowed to happen again.

Aditya and I were woken by a whistling Phandika bringing us a hot cup of tea. He looked cheerful, showing no signs of what had happened the night before except to wink conspiratorially when he collected the pile of axes, kukris and iron bars that lay in my tent. I finished my tea and crawled outside. Babul and Poni were squatting around the fire, cooking breakfast and chatting. They looked up and smiled, a little sheepishly perhaps, but like the old man, they bore no resentment. Life in the elephant camp was back to normal.

There was, however, one problem which was explained to Aditya in hushed tones by a worried Poni and Babul. During the riotous night one of our chickens – the best one, a big plump white cockerel – had disappeared. The reason why this was all being explained so secretively was because of Phandika.

The old fox just loved chicken and nearly always managed to get it on the menu. He would announce firmly and with a hint of regret that a bird had developed a mysterious illness and therefore must be eaten immediately. But so far this chicken had survived. It was obviously his favourite. It travelled in pride of place on top of the jeep and he was often seen feeding it a bit of extra rice or paddy to fatten it up. Babul and Poni were the chicken keepers and would feel the blunt end of Phandika's shoe, or whatever else he could lay his hands on, if he found out. What to do? they had asked Aditya.

The Maratha, true to his race, rose to the occasion and limped off into the depths of Totoland on what I imagined was a dangerous search and destroy mission. About half an hour later I caught him sneaking round the back of the camp clutching a bulging gunny bag. He quickly opened it and our fat feathered friend was returned unnoticed to his roost. I could hardly contain myself.

'What happened?' I asked excitedly.

'Nothing,' he said, shrugging his shoulders. 'I found the chicken in the back of this guy's house and took it.'

'But . . . well, I mean – didn't he react? He *had* stolen it. Didn't he try and stop you?'

'What on earth for,' Aditya said in puzzlement. 'He knew that

I knew that he knew it was my chicken, and that was it. This is India, not England, my friend.'

I shook my head in astonishment. I would never understand this country.

At that moment a forest jeep arrived. The boss was back, and by the force with which she slammed the door, not in a good mood. She stalked into the camp and stood for a moment her face raised like a little animal sensing the air.

'Morning, Parbati.'

'Morning.'

'What happened about the elephant?' I enquired tentatively.

'Tusker,' she replied brusquely. 'Already dead three weeks. Shot by poachers. Ivory missing. Who's been drinking?'

'. . . Well . . . Mark and I had a few last night and . . .'

'Have my boys been drinking?'

'No,' Aditya lied.

'Do not tell me fibs Maratha,' she said. 'I can see it in their faces.'

'Maybe one,' he said nervously ' . . . well, two.'

Parbati grabbed both our arms and frog-marched us to the edge of the camp.

'Do not, I repeat, do not give my young boys booze,' she said, furious. 'They only drink when I give them drink. This is not your camp. They are young. By doing this you will destroy them. I will carry blame. They will become lazy. They will not do their duties. Remember what I tell you, Mark. A lazy mahout is dead mahout. Dino is okay because he has good temperament. But old man is different. Be careful. He is old school mahout. He is hard.'

If only she knew, I thought. We mumbled our apologies.

'Tell Phandika and Dino to get elephants ready,' she commanded. 'We are leaving now.' And after giving instructions to Aditya where to make the next camp, she walked off.

'Have a nice day,' Aditya said, retreating to the safety of the jeep.

13
A Question of Survival

Parbati's mood did not improve on the long ride that day as she pushed the elephants along in almost total silence. The landscape did not help. Apart from a few trees that lined the hot and seemingly endless road, providing a welcome snack for Lakhi and Kanchen, the countryside was monotonous and arid. There was an air of lawlessness – the people appeared unfriendly, suspicious and desperate. I noticed the rotting carcass of a little monkey lying by the side of the road. Bloody stumps disfigured where it had torn its way out of a deadly snare, to crawl away, crippled, to die in agony.

And we were plagued by the flies. I watched in fascination as these greedy winged blood-suckers settled on Kanchen's neck, filled up and droned away, bloated and heavy, avoiding my mis-timed blows. Elephants, I thought, would benefit greatly from the wisdom of Leonardo da Vinci:

> Flies are much attracted by their smell and as they settle on their backs they wrinkle up their skin deepening its tight folds and so kill them.

We stopped once to buy oranges at a weekly market. The air of mistrust and aggression had even pervaded the atmos-phere of these usually jolly and colourful rural supermarkets. An angry mob jostled us and I felt Kanchen vibrate uneasily beneath me.

'Baini, Baini,' I comforted her. And with Phandika roaring and flailing at the crowd below us with his bamboo stick, I brought Kanchen under control and beat a hasty retreat.

'They are angry,' Parbati said. 'Elephant has killed woman nearby. But not only killed,' she added, raising her eyebrows. 'Eaten.'

Gossip and exaggeration are rife in these rural communities. We found later that she had not been eaten but horribly mutilated. The elephant had ripped off both her arms and pulped her head beyond recognition. Hardly a day went by without some gory story of this sort appearing in the local newspapers. It was not surprising. In the Indian elephant, man faces a worthy and intelligent adversary. Apart from its renowned memory, it seemed that it was now capable of feelings of hatred and revenge.

According to Parbati's instructions, Aditya had set up camp on the side of a busy road, next to an airbase. We could scarcely hear ourselves speak above the howl of trucks as they thundered by and the deafening roar of MiG jets above. But again – like everything Parbati did – there was a reason. It was just another example of the elephants' fragile environment. We were in fact right on the border of a national game park.

Exhausted, I dismounted from Kanchen. We had ridden for seven hours, and blood was seeping through the hard callouses on my toes.

'Tomorrow,' Parbati said, 'we will have rest day. We all need it. Particularly my sweeties. We will massage their legs and give *them*', she added pointedly, 'rum for relaxing. But you did good today. That was dangerous situation at the market. You controlled Kanchen well. Good night.' With that she crawled into her tent.

Glory be to God, I thought – praise! I was getting there.

Some rest day it turned out to be. Quite apart from my normal duties, I was made to massage the elephants' legs with a strange and pungent potion and then given a large needle and told to patch up the fraying guddas. And it was a Sunday.

'It is essential always to be busy,' Parbati told me her eyes narrowed in concentration as she deftly shaped the surface of a new scabbard with the aid of a small chisel. She held it up to her eye and grunted in satisfaction. 'You know, when unable to catch elephants because of heavy rains, sometimes we spend weeks just like this.' She then selected one of the little wooden-handled awls that were heating on the embers of the fire and delicately scorched the outline of a little elephant carrying a lotus in its trunk on the smooth surface of the scabbard. 'There,' she said happily, closely scrutinising her handiwork and handing the scabbard over to me. 'This is for you. Does it look like Tara? Soon I will begin on kukri.' She wandered off to check on the elephants.

I was very touched by this gesture and sat admiring the beautiful simplicity of the design. It really did look like Tara. Like elephants, Parbati never failed to surprise you, and one never felt bored in her company. I realised how fond I had become of this remarkable woman as she flitted among us weaving her spells and dispensing her magic like some tiny whimsical sorceress.

In the early afternoon I went to join Phandika and Dino. They were bathing the elephants below the busy road bridge. I paused for a while to enjoy the scene. The bridge shook as the trucks thundered past. Further upstream, judging by the vibrant sounds of modern Hindi film music just audible above the roar of the traffic, a large family on a day out from town was enjoying a picnic. Closer, a small group stood silently around a smouldering pile of ashes. The smell of incense wafted through the air. It was a simple rural cremation. Chanting softly, they gathered the ashes in large tin *thalis* and spread them on the surface of the river.

Like the mélange of orange peel, plastic bags, ashes and dung that were carried by the gentle current beneath me, the picnickers had now joined the mourners and, as if unified by the river, all moved down to watch the elephants.

Lost in my thoughts, I had not noticed the large crowd that had gathered around me.

A scholarly gentleman leaning on a bicycle engaged me in conversation. The cremation, he informed me, was for the remains of the poor woman who had been eaten by the wicked elephant. I shook my head. For here, in front of me, on this peaceful stretch of sun-dappled water the conflict had been innocently portrayed. The picnickers representing the reason – the encroachment of modern

India on rural areas – the elephants the reaction, and the ashes the result.

I scrambled down the embankment where Phandika and Dino had also attracted a crowd. Judging by the handfuls of coins that were being exchanged for the contents of a large sack, they were engaged in some kind of business. Puzzled, I looked inside. It was full of the pumice stones that are used to scrub elephants.

Phandika winked at me. 'Magic stones,' he whispered, tucking a note into his lungi.

In the evening, no doubt wishing to celebrate his new found wealth, Phandika decided that we should dine on chicken. Not any chicken, but special, white, plump cockerel. We had all grown fond of this beautiful bird. It had become our mascot. I pleaded with him, but my pleas fell on deaf ears. He was adamant. The cockerel, he informed me, had developed an unusual throat disease from the ingestion of small stones. It therefore could not breathe.

I bade farewell to my feathered friend. 'Baini, baini,' I whispered, stroking its glossy plumage.

Phandika appeared silently behind me. He was holding a long sharp knife.

'No baini, bandoo. Bye, bye,' he growled happily.

At least Phandika did justice to our departed friend. He produced a delicious dinner. Parbati was in high spirits.

'Tomorrow,' she said, 'you will have proper rest day. I have arranged treat. We will be going into game park on elephants to see rhino, but not on my sweeties. Wildlife laws in India do not allow.' She pointed towards the elephants. 'Anyway, they will have hangover.'

Kanchen and Lakhi, knocked out by the rum we had given them earlier, were lying stretched out on the ground, snoring.

*

Early the next morning we arrived at Jaldapara National Park, home to one of the few remaining populations of the Indian rhinoceros. Outside the Forest Lodge a throng of Indian tourists milled about, waiting for the elephants to take them into the Park.

'We must wait,' Parbati said. 'Come. I want to show you something.'

We entered the lodge. It was a splendid old-fashioned building – its dusty rooms full of lop-sided leather chairs, its wood-panelled walls covered with sun-faded photographs of wildlife.

Parbati stopped in front of a black and white print. 'See,' she said, proudly, 'that is Papa with his favourite elephant – Pratap Singh.'

I took the photograph off the wall and carried it into the light. Her father sat astride a huge elephant, with short, thick tusks. It had picked up a leopard in its trunk and was hurling it contemptuously into the air.

'Wounded leopard,' Parbati said, 'coming to attack Papa. But Pratap saved him.' She pointed to the black discharge running down Pratap's cheeks, 'Pratap was in full musth.' She shook her head sadly. 'They loved each other so much.'

Our elephants had now arrived outside – one for Parbati and me, the other for the film crew. We padded slowly off into the morning mist. It was like entering another world. The dew had created a carpet of diamonds strewn with rubies from the fallen blossoms of the flame-of-the-forest trees.

Parbati was in her element. Enthusiastically she identified the variety of birdlife that surrounded us – doves, kingfishers, different species of mynah and even the elusive imperial green pigeon. I noticed little groups of grass cones hanging from the lower branches of some trees, like miniature rugby balls.

'What are those?' I asked.

'Weaver birds' nests. They are very modern birds. They have electricity.'

'Electricity?!'

She laughed. 'Jungle electricity. According to legend, they catch fire-fly and put on small piece of clay inside their nest. All night their little house is lit up and safe.'

Our elephant soon demonstrated that there is no better all-terrain vehicle. Nor indeed is there any better way of spotting game than from high on its back as it quickly and quietly negotiated slippery, steep paths. In the riverbeds we surprised little groups of barking deer, drinking daintily, and the occasional outraged boar, its back bristling, as it charged away, crashing through the thick undergrowth.

'Bogri,' Parbati said, pointing to a tall bush, swollen with pale yellow berries. Standing up on the elephant's back she stuffed some in her pockets.

'Try one – they are good.'

I grimaced. It was bitter, like a cooking apple.

'You do not like?' she asked, and rustling in a small cotton bag, she produced an apple and a banana.

'You're like a magpie,' I said.

'Magpie,' she said slowly, savouring the word, 'I like that. They are clever bird.'

Leaving the forest behind, we crossed a large open meadow.

'Rhino!' I shouted, pointing at a grey shape in the distance.

She threw up her hands in despair.

'Not rhino, Mark. That is stump. Your eyes are bad. You're not fit for jungle.' She pointed to an area covered by elephant grass. 'We will find rhino there.'

We pushed our way through the tall wavy stems, their edges as sharp as razor blades. In some places the thick grass had been tunnelled through, forming giant burrows.

'Rhino is very clean and tidy animal,' she said. 'He always defecates in same place – at end of tunnel. He does it for good reason. If he soils all grass, he cannot eat.'

We pushed our way through one of the tunnels. At the end, in a small clearing, a pile of dung lay neatly stacked. 'Rhino will defecate here until mound becomes too high. Then he soils buttocks. Only then will he move on. He is creature of habit.'

But it is these habits, Parbati explained, that makes the rhino such easy prey for poachers. Fearing detection from the patrols that try to protect this rare species, poachers seldom use fire-arms. Instead, more deadly and less conspicuous methods have been devised, such as laying electrified wires across the rhino trails or poisoning the salt-licks.

Suddenly the grass exploded in front of us and a rhino

shuffled out, grunting. It stopped for a moment and turned back to stare, wiggling its strange rabbit ears and blinking its piggy eyes. It grunted again and shook its head as though trying to rid itself of the long curved horn attached to the top of its nose. If only it could, I thought, as I gazed at this strange, shy and harmless creature, its body encased in panelled armour, like a Samurai warrior. Its fabled horn, made of hair, fetches thousands of dollars a kilo when reduced to a powder. In the macabre and traditional medicinal markets of the Orient it will be ground up, along with the bones of that other most endangered animal, the tiger, to produce a priceless potion which is believed to enhance sexual prowess.

India does not exactly help to explode this myth. A retired game warden had informed me that rhino urine was being sold for four rupees a bottle in the zoos in Assam as a cure for sexual impotency. Quite simply, if the Chinese are allowed to continue to trade in animal products, they will work their way through what remains of India's wildlife.

It was a sobering thought, and became more so when we arrived back. News had filtered through that a rhino calf had been found on the other side of the park – murdered for two and a half inches of this legendary horn.

We rode back to the Park pilkhana. As we dismounted Parbati asked if I liked the elephant we had ridden.

'One of the best,' I replied, remembering its speed and sure-footedness.

'It was bought last year at Sonepur,' she told me. 'I advised Forestry Department. Look at her front feet and count toenails.'

I knelt down. To my surprise there were only sixteen. According to the ancient Sanskrit elephant texts, no one in their right mind bought a sixteen-toed elephant. It was considered extremely inauspicious.

She laughed. 'Like Kanchen with her pale eyes, eh? Remember? And they got her cheap.'

After a moment's pause she continued: 'There is something else, Mark, something I meant to tell you. I look at your book again. In it someone tells you mukhnas [tuskless males] are bad elephants. This is quite incorrect. Mukhnas are good elephant. They are quiet and trustworthy. My papa used them many times for mela shikar. Next time when you write book on elephants, ask me.'

As we entered the pilkhana, I remembered a piece from P. D. Stracey's book, *Elephant Gold*:

There is something about the atmosphere and smell of a pilkhana which is subtly exciting – that typical but not unpleasant smell of burning elephant dung and refuse combined with the sweet resinous odour of crushed elephant grass; the sight of the straight rows of standings and the smooth tethering posts to which are tied the restless captives, shaking their ears and swinging their tails while they eat.

I agreed with him, except that in our case the restive captives were not standing, shaking their ears and swinging their tails while they ate. They were straining against the ropes that tied them to their tethering posts, bellowing, squeaking and grunting as they waited impatiently for their mothers to arrive back from the forest with their food. Instinctively I rushed towards them. Parbati yelled a warning, but it was too late. I found out the hard way that, even at this age, baby elephants are remarkably strong. I was butted in the stomach by one of these bundles of trouble and sent sprawling. Parbati laughed and helped me to my feet. She was surrounded by a group of small children. Clearly she was worshipped around here and, like the Pied Piper, they trailed behind her wherever she went.

Baby elephants look older when they are young than when they reach maturity. With their wizened features, pointed bushy beards and exploding eyebrows, from under which their beady little eyes glower fiercely, they look like a bunch of angry dwarves. Here each one had already developed its own character. There was the bully, always pushing and butting; the playful and curious one, exploring the delights of Aditya's camera bag; and the shy one, standing tentatively alone, longing to join in but not daring.

There was a cry of delight from the children. I turned round.

Trotting behind a forest officer and attached to a piece of rope was a round, wet, furry conker, wearing little white slippers. It was a tiny calf, perhaps only a month or so old, fresh from its bath, still bearing the auburn bristles of babyhood, the soles of its soft feet pale and plump. Parbati and I squatted down in front of it. Immediately it sensed food at hand for Parbati's pockets were filled with berries. But there was a problem – how to get them. At this young age, the muscles in an elephant's trunk are not fully developed. Grunting in frustration, it swung its little trunk round and round, as if trying to rid itself of this useless appendage. Parbati giggled and, delving into her pockets, produced a handful of berries and gently hand-fed the baby.

By now the other elephants had returned, bearing huge loads of fodder on their backs. Grunting and squeaking, the calves rushed excitedly around, entangling themselves in their mothers' legs. The fodder was unloaded and the mahouts divided it into small individual piles. The calves were now in a frenzy. Each family's pile seemed to be bigger and better than their own, and the calves rushed from one to the other, unable to make up their minds. The fodder had now attracted other potential diners. Soon ducks were chasing pigeons, chickens were chasing ducks and they were all being chased by the baby elephants. Towering above them, their mothers looked down, occasionally reprimanding the babies by cuffing them with their trunks or pushing them gently aside with their legs.

I felt a soft, wet nudge against my cheek. 'What about this little fellow?' I asked Parbati. 'Where's his mother?'

'He does not have one,' she said sadly, and explained that it had been found lying at the bottom of a *nullah*, injured and weak from hunger. The Forestry Department had brought it in, otherwise it would have died.

'In old days,' she told me, 'this would not have happened. Often we find abandoned calves that had fallen into ditch or pits, lost and confused when roving males chased mothers on heat. We would help calf, and herd would always come back and look after. Now all is different. More and more, we find deserted calves. Sometimes we find in tea gardens – separated from herd

when villagers drive them out. Just near here there is forestry place
where there are six tiny ones which have been abandoned.'

'But don't the mothers come back?' I asked.

'How can they come back?' she replied. 'They would be shot.
They will not take risk any more. They have to move on to
protect rest of herd. There is no forest in which to hide. They
have no choice.'

It was unimaginable. The ferocious devotion mothers nor-
mally show to their offspring is legendary. I had heard of an
elephant attacking a train which had knocked down her baby,
pummelling the engine until it could no longer run. Now, it
seems, traumatised parents are simply unable to look after their
offspring if they cannot keep up with the rest of the herd. The
natural instinct of this most family-oriented of animals has been
compromised so much that its very psyche could be changing.

I realised as we watched the little calves wallowing happily
around in the water, enjoying their bath, that it is not only
the wild elephant that fights for its survival – the domesticated
elephant also faces a crisis. What does the future hold for these
little creatures and hundreds like them all over the country? The
demand for captive elephants is declining now, and will be less in
ten or twelve years' time when these calves will be big enough
to start work. Massive deforestation throughout Asia is making
working elephants redundant as machines take over their traditional role in timber extraction.

In 1988, when I arrived at Sonepur with Tara, more than
two hundred elephants were there and business was brisk. When
I returned three years later, there were sixty-eight elephants.
Most of them went home unsold. What will happen to them?
Some will go to temples, some will work in game parks, and
some will be bought by rich individuals as symbols of status
and good luck. One or two very lucky ones could even end
up like Tara.

It was ironic, I thought, that encompassed in this one animal
are all the best characteristics – beauty, intelligence, strength,
peacefulness, wisdom, bravery and compassion, but because of
two other noble attributes – namely size and longevity – we

will not allow it to survive. It has become a victim of its own creation.

It was on to Parbati's narrow shoulders that I unloaded all my fears. She shrugged wearily. 'We can only continue to do our best for them. We need miracle.'

14

In the Company of Elephants

I t was a miracle of a different kind that we encountered beside the
busy road we were riding along the next morning. A five-legged
cow. It was a splendidly stupid animal, caparisoned in a red cloth
through which its perfectly formed fifth limb protruded strangely
from its side. Bells hung around its neck, and it wore an ornate
headdress of beads, shells and lucky coins mounted in silver. It
was attached to its owner – a slippery sort of character, sporting
an expensive-looking silver wristwatch – by a thin cord that passed
through the cow's nostrils like the bit on a horse's bridle.

'Get down and make wish,' Parbati told me.

'To a cow?' I replied suspiciously. 'Are you sure?'

'Of course. Cows are sacred to us. Particularly five-legged
one.'

Reluctantly I clambered down from Kanchen and approached
this holy and auspicious beast. Both owner and cow gazed at me
implacably.

'What do I do?'

'You make wish first,' Parbati explained. 'If cow accepts,
cow will nod.'

'And then?'

'You hold out your fists. If cow turns around and then licks
fist, wish will come true.'

The inevitable small crowd had gathered, and I was feeling
decidedly self-conscious. It was a ridiculous scenario. A foreigner

standing on the side of a busy main road in India, talking to a five-legged cow.

'Parbati,' I asked, 'can I – just sort of – whisper in its ear?'

'You can try,' she replied, 'but nothing will be done without money.'

I handed over a coin. The owner looked at it disdainfully. I quickly bent down and whispered into the cow's large, velvety ear. It shook its head. For a moment I saw stars as its horn cracked against my skull. I glared at the cow and its owner. They glared back at me. Clearly this propitious pair had expected richer pickings. I remounted Kanchen and rubbed my head.

'What did you wish?' Parbati asked, laughing.

'None of your business; it's a secret.'

'But I am your guru,' she replied playfully. 'You must tell all.'

'Well, I'm not going to. A secret is a secret. You wouldn't tell me, would you?'

'Ah, but that is different. I am woman.'

The traffic became heavier and heavier and we moved in a constant cloud of thick, black, choking fumes. We cut off the road down a steep escarpment and crossed the mighty Torsa river, aptly named 'angry water', as it thundered down from the hills of Bhutan, shaking even the mighty legs of the great beasts that forced their way across below us.

We camped that night on the banks of a small tributary. It was Aditya's birthday. He was forty-five.

'Nobody remembers,' he said mournfully, as we sat naked in the cool water, sipping rum.

Something rumbled behind us. We turned in alarm. Towering above us in the gloom stood Kanchen and Lakhi. 'Happy Birthday Aditya' was written across their broad foreheads in brightly coloured chalks. Somebody had remembered.

*

We pushed on steadily eastwards. Christmas came and went, and so did the forest. That was replaced by plantations of quick cash crops – sal, eucalyptus and teak – providing good and easy revenue for the government, but nothing for the elephants. Conservation was well advertised in these areas by curious poems written on little green boards. I particularly liked one, a stanza written in 1930 by General George Pope-Morris:

> Woodman, spare that tree!
> Touch not a single bough!
> In youth it sheltered me
> And I'll protect it now.

Monkeys, however, did not pay much attention to Morris's wise words. Passing under some trees in one of the few pockets of forest, Kanchen and I and Phandika were nearly flattened by a large branch which crashed down beside us. I looked up. A group of primates were chattering noisily in the thick foliage.

'Bloody hooligans,' I shouted. 'They're destroying the forest.'

'Not at all, Mark,' Parbati explained. 'Man should learn from his ancestors. Look at that branch. It is dead, full of termites. If they do not remove it, termites will spread and kill tree.'

My natural history lesson continued. Again, it was due to monkeys or, more precisely, a fruit named after them – the monkey-fruit – known locally as the *bandrahola*. Tempted by one of these juicy pods that resembled large, hairy caterpillars, I reached out my hand.

'Do not touch, Mark,' Parbati shouted in alarm. 'When fruit bursts, hair is like needles. You will itch and burn for fifteen days. There is no cure. Even elephants, if they touch them, go mad. There is a saying we have about bandrahola. If you have man who goes astray, apply bandrahola and he will stay.'

'What about women?' I asked.

She smiled.

I should have tried it for Parbati went astray for the next few days. She had been called out again by the Forestry Department to track down an elephant that had been spotted with a steel snare clamped on to its trunk.

That night, while we were sitting around the campfire, I asked Phandika if he had ever seen the Gaja-Mukta, the fabled elephant pearl, supposedly found in the heads of elephants. He tapped his mug on a log in the fire. Aditya carefully poured out a small measure. Considering our last experience, we were not taking any chances. He drank deeply and smacked his lips.

He told us that Gaja-Mukta is only found in certain elephants. In God-elephants, he called them, which are like spirits. One minute they are there, the next they are gone. He had seen only one God-elephant, a single-tusker, when he was working in a neighbouring state. The people there knew it was a God-elephant. They killed it and split its skull. Inside was Gaja-Mukta. It was big and sparkled like a diamond.

I asked Parbati about this a few days later.

She told me the old fox was probably drunk. Her father had worked with elephants for over fifty years and had never seen or heard of it. However, she remembered him telling her that once, while cleaning out the soft substance found in the hollow root of a dead elephant's tusk, he had found a small white object, about one-and-a-half inches long, formed from calcium. Perhaps, she suggested, the legend had sprung from similar findings.

On the other hand, Phandika may not have been drunk. There are many references to the Gaja-Mukta in books recording the history of the ancient kingdom of Kamarupa, now known as Assam. One states that:

Ratnapala was a war-like and powerful prince and that, by reason of the elephant pearls carried forth by the impetus of the unstrainable stream of blood running from the split foreheads of the elephants of his enemy, his, Ratnapala's battlefield, looked beautiful, like a marketplace strewn with the stones of merchants and ruby-coloured through the blood of the slain.

And an inscription on an early copper plate relates:

He is victorious in the battlefield, adorned by the garland made of the pearls strewn from the heads of the elephants killed in battle.

Like Bhim, my old mahout, Phandika believed in many legends and, like Bhim, it did not seem to matter whether it was fact or fiction. He considered the elephant was of the highest caste – a Brahmin – and ruled over all men. At one time, many many years ago, he told us, the elephant committed a sin. The caste order was reversed and that is why man now rides the elephant.

Humans, he continued, have now committed a much bigger sin – they have destroyed the elephants' home. But, he believed, the elephants' time was coming again. They would go berserk. How many guns could man fire at them? How many crackers could they explode? The next four years, he announced, would be like Armageddon.

Armageddon was closer than Phandika thought, as we discovered later that night. Kanchen and Lakhi were nervous. We could hear them fidgeting and rattling their chains in the gloom.

'Haathi close,' Phandika told us, and he threw the beam of his torch towards the elephants. I nearly jumped out of my skin. Thirty pairs of eyes stared at me from the gloom.

'Elephants,' I shouted.

'Relax, you fool,' Aditya said, 'they are only fireflies.'

There was some justification for my alarm. In the weak beam of the torch, the green luminosity of the fireflies exactly matched the colour of the elephants' eyes.

About half an hour later my fears were vindicated. A terrible hullabaloo erupted close by, as Kanchen and Lakhi bellowed in alarm. Phandika switched on his torch, illuminating a scene of bedlam. There were now three elephants in the pilkhana and one was clearly not welcome. Clumsily it tried to climb on to Kanchen's back.

Phandika laughed. 'Kanchen pik-pik.'

Clearly Kanchen was not in the mood for 'pik-pik', and trumpeting with rage, she drove off the rampant Romeo into the night.

Aditya and I were shaken by this fracas, but Phandika and Dino continued their drinking as if nothing had happened. We settled back uneasily around the fire.

'You know, when I was a kid,' Aditya said, 'I used to catch fireflies and put them in my tent at night.'

'I suppose you were afraid of the dark?'

'Of course not,' he replied testily. 'Marathas are never afraid. It was just lovely to lie there, like we are now, and the bigger the firefly the better. Like those,' he said, pointing to two large green orbs suspended in the dark behind Phandika. We looked closer.

'Phandika!'

The old man moved like lightning. He picked up a burning log and in one movement whirled round and threw it. It arced like a fireball and hit Romeo squarely between the eyes, sending him squealing back into the gloom in a cloud of sparks.

He squatted back down beside the fire, 'Punk,' he growled. 'No respect.'

★

Parbati returned early next morning, unable to locate the snared elephant. As we rode along another busy road, I told her what had happened. She laughed.

'You were lucky. It was young foolish elephant. One time Phandika and me were driving elephants back with torches. Phandika threw torch at big elephant who picked it up and threw it back. We were very surprised.'

Not as surprised as the two men who were sitting cross-legged on the edge of a tall stone bridge spanning a river as we crossed. Their heads were down, deep in conversation. Silently we passed them. They looked up. Shock registered across their faces and, moving backwards, they fell straight off the edge of the bridge. Parbati and I dismounted, worried lest they were hurt. It was a long drop. We scrambled down the escarpment to find two very wet men standing on the bank, grinning in embarrassment. They fumbled in their pockets, took out some coins and handed them to Parbati.

'For Ganesh,' they explained. 'He has saved our lives.'

We spent our new-found wealth on tea, oranges and biscuits in a little shop while waiting for a steam train to pass at a small town called Rajabhatkhawa – literally meaning 'the king's dining-room'. According to legend, it was here that the King of Bhutan dined with the King of the Koch, now known as Cooch Behar, to celebrate the end of the wars that had raged between them for many years.

Leaving the town behind us, we cut across country, skirting vast fields of mustard ablaze with yellow. Dotted here and there, like oases in a desert, were little villages, barely visible through the luxuriance of the bamboo and plantain groves that surrounded them.

We dipped in and out of the patches of forest, finally emerging on to a flat, sandy clearing through which a river ran swiftly. Ahead of us lay an uninterrupted curtain of green – the Buxa Tiger Reserve.

It was a beautiful day. Parbati and I decided to stretch our legs while Phandika and Dino took the elephants on ahead. We walked along the riverbed. The air was sweet and scented. Wild lemons grew in abundance among the thick bushes which lined the riverbank. Overhead the still air was disturbed as a pair of giant Indian hornbills launched themselves awkwardly from a tree and flapped away like pterodactyls, uttering an inane and raucous cry which Mr Salim Ali, the great Indian ornithologist, describes as 'a chicken being seized by a cook'.

In the far distance, on the other side of the river, we caught a glimpse of purple. Aditya was setting up the frog. We reached the river, its broad expanse glinting dully, like polished iron, in the evening sun.

Gallantly, I offered to carry Parbati across. She leapt on to my back, dug her toes into my sides and shouted 'Agit.'

I now knew what Kanchen had to suffer.

'You are doing right thing by carrying me, Mark,' Parbati said happily, as I slithered and lurched through the icy torrent. 'God will smile on you. You will be nearer to achieving goal.'

At that moment, my only goal was to get across the river as fast as possible. She hitched herself higher on my back, nearly knocking us both into the water.

'I will tell you story. One time guru and chela were wondering how to cross deep river, just like us, to worship god in temple over other side. Chela was wanting to please guru. Just like you. Chela offers to carry guru on his back across river. God sees them and thinks, look at that devotion. They are crossing deep river, just to worship me. Then god thinks, I wonder who is more devoted – guru or chela. Finally they arrive at temple. God says to guru, "Your chela has risked life and limb to carry you across. His devotion is greater." So you see,' she said, slipping from my back as I struggled on to the bank, 'even guru to reach god needs chela. But do not let your head become swollen,' she warned. 'Remember who is boss.'

Aditya had organised a perfect camp. It was just like the old days. Incense burned on banana leaves in our tents and bottles of beer were chilling in the cool waters of the river. Phandika and Dino had indulged in some serious deforestation, and the results had been carried and stacked neatly by Kanchen and Lakhi. We bathed in the glow of a setting sun, tainted by a thin plume of smoke which drifted upwards from the funnel of a little steam engine that puffed its way over a bridge in the distance.

Later, as we huddled around the fire, a domed sky, studded with stars, enveloped us snugly like a giant tent. I felt that all I had to do was to walk to the perimeter of the camp, pull back the flap and step out into infinity.

'Tomorrow,' Parbati said, 'I will show you mela shikar. It was here, maybe fifteen years ago, I caught Lakhi.'

'And it is here, the day after tomorrow,' Aditya added, 'that we're going to celebrate.'

Only two days to New Year's Eve.

15
Indian Rope Tricks

'From this we will make ropes for mela shikar,' Parbati said. 'See how soft it is.'

In the dawn light the contents of that other enormous suitcase in Parbati's tent, the one that had tantalised me for so long, were at last revealed. Neatly tied bundles of pure jute.

I ran a thin strand through my fingers. It was like silken hair.

'My papa always used jute – it is strong but more important, soft and therefore does not injure skin of elephants.'

In *Elephant Gold*, P. D. Stracey wrote:

The case of the 'owner-rider' is rare, most of the owners being staid or middle-aged individuals. But there are one or two notable exceptions. One of them, most surprisingly, was the son of a rajah. 'Lalji', as we called him . . . took to mela shikar with his phandis for the sheer sport of it. He was a born elephant man with a deep love for the animal and a most humane approach to the sometimes sordid business of elephant catching. He could always be relied upon to observe the rules scrupulously and had great control over his men, with whom he lived in the jungle.

For two hours I sat watching Parbati and Phandika prepare the ropes. They worked silently and quickly, totally engrossed as they weaved, plaited and twisted – memories flooding back as the familiar rhythms flowed through their hands.

Miraculously, what hours before had been a spaghetti-like tangle of threads, had now been transformed into two long thick ropes. One, which Parbati explained was called a *phand*, would be used as a lasso and attached to the other, the *phara*, which would be wound around the chest of the *koonki* (mounted elephant) like a broad belt.

'Pick up phand,' she ordered. I gasped. It was heavy, *really* heavy. Parbati laughed. 'See, it is not like cowboys. We are catching elephants not cows.'

The tensity and strength of both the ropes was then tested in the ultimate and most logical way. Phandika tied one end around a tree, and gave the other end to Lakhi. On command she dug in her back legs and pulled . . . and pulled. The rope stretched, but held firm. Parbati was satisfied.

On the way back to camp my feet were suddenly swept from under me and I lay on the ground like a trussed turkey. Parbati stood over me, holding the end of the phand. She pulled slightly and the rope tightened around my ankles.

She laughed. 'Good rope. Strong but soft.'

Not a bad self-description I thought as I untangled the ropes and struggled to my feet.

Over breakfast she told me about mela shikar. A camp would be set up in the jungle, from which each day people would be sent out to establish the movement of the herds. All food was carried in bamboo tubes and sacks. Metal items were kept to a minimum as unnatural sounds would carry through the jungle. Washing was forbidden and all clothing was rubbed in the ground. During the actual capture the phandis and mahouts would smear themselves with elephant dung and wear only loin-cloths.

On the fast, strong and fearless koonkies, the phandi and mahout would quietly approach the herd. The phandi would then select his quarry – usually a small elephant between four and six feet at the shoulder. Big elephants were avoided unless there was a special demand. The danger was too great.

Their smell camouflaged by the dung, the team were able to guide the koonki right up alongside their prospective captive. As long as they kept absolutely quiet there was no danger of detection. Elephants are short-sighted and rarely look up. With extreme caution the phandi would lean over and drop the noose on to the neck of the elephant, placing it so that the upper part lay on the neck and the lower section hung on the trunk. This was most important. Herein lies the irony of mela shikar; for in its effort to protect its most prized possession, the elephant immediately retracts its trunk and allows itself to be noosed.

Then all hell breaks loose as the elephant bellows in protest and strains against the tightening rope. At this point a skilled phandi really shows his worth. Like a big-game fisherman fighting a marlin, he plays the elephant, reeling it in then letting out slack, always exerting just the right pressure. Too heavy a touch could cause strangulation, too light a lost prize.

For a very strong elephant extra koonkies will be brought in and more nooses deployed. The koonkies can also be used to drive off the rest of the herd if they come to the rescue. This happened, Parbati added, when Lakhi was caught. Two big females charged and they were lucky to escape injury because the koonkies intervened.

I asked her why she had chosen Lakhi.

'She is right size,' she said. 'But I like something else. I see it in her eyes. She is playful elephant – I like that. Now you catch your *own* elephant.'

We were in a nice flat clearing among tall grass. Mounted on Lakhi's broad shoulders, wearing my own comfortable clothes, not half-naked and covered in elephant dung, swearing and gesticulating instead of keeping silent, and patiently guided by Phandika, the world champion, I attempted to throw a noose over Kanchen who was grazing just below me.

'You are just not used to it, Mark,' Parbati said kindly.

My arms aching with fatigue, my hands rigid with cramp, I threw the phand and watched in despair as it landed in a tangled knot for the fortieth time on top of Kanchen's head.

'Here, let me show you,' she said. She danced up Lakhi's trunk and settled in front of me.

She rearranged the ropes and, lifting herself up, deftly flicked out the noose. I watched in admiration and jealousy as it arced to land in the perfect position on Kanchen's head and trunk. Immediately Kanchen curled up her nose and the noose fell neatly around her neck. Parbati dismounted and told me to try again. Exactly the same thing happened as before. Eventually it was Kanchen who saved me from total humiliation. Tired of being used as a prize in a hoopla stall, she reached up and pulled the noose over her head. I quickly pulled on the rope and tightened it. I was elated. I had captured my first elephant. My efforts received a small but polite smattering of applause. Even the old fox clapped me on the back.

'Shabash, shabash,' he growled sarcastically . . . 'Phandika!'

Only Aditya, who had been waiting all day to record this momentous event, remained unimpressed. He informed me that if I intended to pursue my career in movies I should not audition for westerns.

On the way back to camp, Parbati stressed the importance of reintroducing mela shikar, particularly in this area. In India the capture of wild elephants had been banned since 1981. Many experts, she said, were still against capture, maintaining that it breaks down the genetic pool. While in the past this argument may have been relevant, now there is no alternative. She explained that a mix of modern and traditional methods should be employed. By using tranquillisation during capture, the risk of injury to elephants would be greatly reduced. Afterwards the animals could either be domesticated or translocated to a more suitable habitat.

I thought about what Parbati had said as we rode on. Undoubtedly it was the correct solution, but in reality it offered only a temporary answer to the problem. India now faces the ultimate conundrum – a Catch-22 situation. As the demand for captive elephants diminishes, the number of wild elephants increases. As the population multiplies, the space minimises. What on earth, I wondered, was India going to do with her elephants?

At camp, the figure sitting cross-legged in the opening of Parbati's tent, pouting into a small mirror, dispelled my gloomy thoughts.

'Oh bloody humbug! Not him,' Parbati groaned.

'*She*', I remarked, 'would be more apt.' I observed this apparition blow daintily on his fingernails which he had decorated in a delicate shade of pink.

'I do not know what to do with him,' she said. 'He lives on tea estate where I work. He will not leave me alone. He is always taking my beauty products. He tells me if I will not use them, he will. Now I use him as sort of servant or', she giggled, 'maybe maidservant.'

It was a most incongruous and farcical situation as this painted puppet dressed in a décolleté dayglo top and skimpy satin shorts, minced around the rough and tumble of the elephant camp, flirting outrageously. Aditya hit the nail on the head. He was, he stated, an elephant groupie. Fortunately his groupie activities were limited to domestic chores. To divert his attentions Parbati had ordered him to springclean our tents.

Suddenly he cried, 'Eeek!'

He was standing on tiptoe, his hands clasped in horror, staring down beside Aditya's tent. We rushed over. Coiled on the ground, hissing angrily, was a large snake.

'Stand back!' roared Aditya, '*ophiophagus hannah* – it's the king cobra.'

'King cobra,' Parbati said scornfully. Unsheathing her kukri, she neatly lopped its head off and threw the remains in the bushes. 'It is rat snake. They eat frogs too.' Pointing at Aditya's tent, she laughed uproariously at her own joke.

*

The next day we set off by jeep to the nearby town of Cooch Behar to stock up on provisions – particularly alcohol – for it was New Year's Eve.

Parbati took us to the old palace, the former seat of the Maharajah of Cooch Behar. As a child she had often accompanied her father, who, apart from being a family friend, supplied the ruler with elephants. We entered through rusting ornate iron gates. On either side, crowning tall pitted pillars, a magnificent elephant and a roaring lion stood defiant – a poignant reminder of grander days. In the distance the palace loomed majestically out of the morning mist. The grounds had now become public property: people squatted and defecated while others washed in the brackish rainwater of the still fountains.

Parbati shook her head. 'Once all this was lovely park. Full of flowers and trees. At gate there were sentry boxes. Guards stood to attention in beautiful uniforms.' We weaved our way through the herds of cows grazing on the weeds in the flowerbeds. 'I remember', she continued, 'counting over one hundred elephants in royal pilkhana.'

I gazed up at the crumbling facade, now the home of parakeets and mynahs, squabbling in their nests in the broken masonry. Windows were replaced by boards. The brickwork was defaced with graffiti. High above us, the magnificent cupola glittered in the morning sun.

'Indo-Saracenic architecture,' said Aditya.

As it was once home to Hindu royalty, I was a little sceptical. Still, he did have a point. The strange mish-mash of architecture was not unlike the old west pier in Brighton – and just as empty, sad and deserted. When we wandered round the back, it appeared that someone, apart from the birds, was taking advantage of its former glory and magnificence. Above a small pink out-building hung a little sign – 'Queen's Lady Beauty Parlour – the Palace Compound'. We stepped inside.

Curiously, apart from a pink sink, a mirror and a couple of chairs, the room was dominated by a large colour poster of the Argentinian tennis player Gabriella Sabatini. The puzzle was soon solved by the arrival of the proprietor of this establishment – a small, fit, Nepalese gentleman, who turned out to be the former tennis marker. This building had once been the tennis pavilion and had been donated to him by the late Maharajah. The marker's wife now ran a thriving little business. We perused the bewildering list of services on offer. Plain U, long-step, short-step, boy-cut, blunt-cut, temporary coiling, perming, perming-half, perming full. There were even more puzzling treats: temporary outlining; threading (eyebrow, upperlip, forehead); facials (plain or herbal); waxing (hands, full-leg, half leg); manicure; pedicure with polish; and brindle makeup. You could also get yourself bleached – 'Kardal fairness', a small sign advertised, 'it makes you visibly fairer in minutes'.

'Just think,' I said to Aditya, 'in minutes you could become an English gentleman.'

'Speaking of gentlemen,' he retorted, 'you could do with a shave and a haircut. You look like a bloody hippy.'

'Sorry dear,' I lisped. 'It's just impossible. Continuity problems.'

But Parbati *did* want a haircut. She was looking with interest at the sixteen different styles on offer. Aditya and I quickly dissuaded her – she was blessed with the most beautiful hair. We suggested instead that she have a manicure, pedicure, herbal facial, and those bat wings of eyebrows plucked a little. She emerged looking radiant.

In a liquor store we stocked up with a new brand of beer – Dansburg – and a new whisky evocatively named Bhutan Mist. At a nearby market I purchased a handsome black and tan cockerel. With its red comb sprouting proudly from its head, it somehow (no disrespect intended), reminded me of my old friend, the photographer Don McCullin, after one of his DIY haircuts. Coincidentally, I had just received news that he had been awarded the CBE. In his honour I christened my new feathered companion Donald McCullin CBE.

At a more modern establishment I offered Parbati a New Year present. For an hour-and-a-half she flitted hesitantly, fingering bolts of iridescent silk and rummaging through piles of colourful shawls.

'You must choose for me,' she said eventually.

Aditya and I settled on a black and gold tartan-patterned shawl. We told her it matched her eyes. She was delighted.

We arrived back in the camp in the late afternoon. Parbati went straight off with the elephants to collect fodder. I offered to join her.

'No, no,' she said. 'Tonight is New Year. I must cut for my sweeties.'

With the help of the boys and Parbati's maidservant we prepared the camp for the party. The crew would be joining us. We built a big fire and erected a make-shift bar from the guddas. When they returned with the elephants, I presented Dino and Phandika with the shoes I had bought in the Harrods of Mal Bazar. Dino was delighted, but Phandika was more interested in the chicken.

It turned out to be a riotous night. We dined on Donald McCullin CBE, drank Dansburg and Bhutan Mist and danced like dervishes. In the early hours of the morning I collapsed beside Aditya, who, like us all, was slightly the worse for wear. The only one still on her feet was Parbati, whirling endlessly, her bangles flashing in the firelight like some gypsy queen.

'Wild Thing,' Aditya slurred and passed out.

16

A Chapter of Accidents

I awoke late with a terrible hangover and made my New Year's resolution. I would give up alcohol.

It was not to last long. I heard the clink of glass outside my tent. I crawled slowly outside, shading my eyes against the hideous glare of the bright sun.

'Good morning,' Aditya said brightly, patting the cloth bag which hung over his shoulder. 'Hair of the dog? Oh, by the way, happy New Year.'

We found a perfect spot – a sandy bank shaded by mango trees overlooking the river. Sipping our beer we watched the village women emerging from the forest in a colourful procession, carrying enormous bundles of timber on their heads.

I started to count them, but soon gave up. I turned to Aditya, 'Can you imagine how much wood has passed us in the last hour? And this must happen every single day of the year. They're literally carrying away the forest. Do you realise', I added pompously, 'that sixty per cent of your domestic fuel is firewood? No wonder the elephants have nowhere to go.'

'It's all very well for you, or anybody else, to say that. These are poor people. How else can they cook and feed their families and keep their children warm at night. By the way,' he added, 'we haven't exactly set a good example. Think of our fires.'

We were interrupted by a flurry of wings just above us. Looking up, I saw a pair of large rust-coloured ducks with pretty pale yellow heads swoop down and land in the water further upstream.

'Ruddy sheldrake,' Aditya said, 'or Brahmini ducks. At least the villagers are better off than them.'

'What on earth do you mean?'

He laughed. 'It's just a legend. A god put a curse on them. They must always part at night.'

*

It was about parting that Parbati talked that night. We were now nearing the border of Assam. Parbati had received news that conditions along our proposed route had deteriorated and she could not take the risk. Our journey was to be cut short. I was bitterly disappointed.

'It is sad for me too, Mark,' she said. 'More than anything I would like to show you big elephant herds and big forests. But cheer up, guru will not let you down. I still have few tricks up my sleeve.'

Distracted, she said, 'Rain is coming soon.'

I looked up. The moon gleamed palely through a strange diaphanous halo.

'See, she has water in her mouth.'

*

The next day we entered the cathedral silence of Buxa Tiger Reserve. I should have been happy. For the first time, I was witnessing a perfectly preserved elephant habitat. But I felt weak and lethargic. Perhaps it was fatigue, or perhaps it was the thought that our journey would soon end. My listlessness communicated itself to Kanchen and she exploited me mercilessly, wandering from side to side, enjoying at leisure the abundance and variety of food on offer.

Phandika did his best to cheer me up. He even composed a special song about an Englishman who comes to India and becomes his brother mahout.

Here the forest really bared her fangs, sucking us greedily into the green maw of her mouth as we padded silently down long, wet, misty tunnels. We dipped in and out of the mist; eerie will-o-the-wisps blew up from nowhere and the trees groaned and sighed, as if in warning; the elephants became edgy, grumbling, wheezing and entwining their trunks for reassurance.

Piles of fresh elephant dung dotted the tracks and the high wet banks were pitted and scarred where the herds had gouged out and eaten the red earth, rich with essential minerals.

The deeper we went into the forest, the deeper I sank into depression. A sharp poke in the ribs, followed by a hoarse garlic and rum-laced whisper, informed me that the brother mahout had no balls and was not worthy of Kanchen. I was told to get off and walk. I glanced across at Parbati. She remained silent and inscrutable behind those dark glasses. Reluctantly I dismounted. Crestfallen, I followed on foot behind. But he was right – my behaviour was unacceptable. For people like him, life is hard and unrelenting. One just gets on and deals with it.

I did not have to walk for long. In the distance we could hear the roar of a revving engine. We reached a break in the forest. In the soft sand of a dried-up riverbed the jeep had become bogged down, its back wheels spinning to no avail. Parbati deployed the elephants and in minutes they had effortlessly extracted their modern successor.

We made camp under a square of silk cotton trees, hemmed in by thick jungle. We were now deep in the core area of the wildlife reserve.

'Any chance of seeing a tiger?' I asked Parbati.

She laughed. 'At least tiger experts. But maybe we will see elephants. This is real camp, just like old days with my papa. We must light small fires not only for our safety but for my sweeties. Kanchen is on heat. Now I will take bath. I need six bottles of beer.' She laughed at my bewilderment. 'Not for drinking, for shampoo. It is excellent for hair.'

She picked her way down to the river, carrying her bottles and singing. She really was extraordinary.

While Parbati took her bath, a group of women filed through the camp, carrying bamboo palanquins overflowing with forest produce. They were exquisitely beautiful, with pale skins, high cheekbones and big dark slanting eyes.

'Meche tribals,' Aditya said. 'You can tell by their skin. They're descended from the Bodos, the indigenous people of Assam. We're near the border now. You'll find the women will become fairer and prettier.'

Parbati returned from her bath – shiny, sleek and perfumed like a brewery.

'Where is Phandika?' she asked.

'He's gone to collect some stones for the stove,' Aditya replied.

'Old fox,' she laughed knowingly. 'It's just excuse. You wait. He is chasing women. He will be gone long time. He will tell me he had to go far into jungle to find suitable stones.'

Half an hour later, Phandika struggled back to the camp under a load of heavy stones. He dropped them noisily and, gesticulating theatrically, informed us that this was a very bad place to camp. He had walked four miles to find them.

Parbati smiled. 'You see, that's why I've eaten twenty-eight fox heads.'

Her divinations did not end there. She was right – the moon had been drinking water. It now burst and heavy rain began to fall. The campsite soon resembled a muddy English farmyard. Parbati ordered the boys to dig small trenches around the tents to ease the torrential flow of water that was beginning to pour through the camp as the nearby river rapidly filled up and overflowed.

I retreated to my tent but it was not much better in there. Frayed and torn from the wear and tear of the journey, it had developed leaks, and I paddled around on my lilo. Aditya faced a worse predicament. The frog, due to its lightness, kept breaking its moorings and floating away, bobbing like a little purple balloon on the river of mud. Eventually, we took it down and Aditya moved in with me. Parbati, however, seemed quite at home.

'You should be used to this,' she said, sitting like a wet jewel, stirring a pot over the fire, protecting herself with a large banana leaf. 'In England it always rains, does it not?'

I noticed that the fire was beginning to fizzle out. Feeling guilty,

I scrambled out into the rain and pulled a dry log from under a tarpaulin. I was about to throw it on the fire when Parbati stopped me.

'You must always obey rules of forest, Mark,' she explained. 'All wood is sacred. Many things, sometimes dangerous things, live in here. Before you sacrifice wood to fire, you must give them chance to escape.'

She unsheathed her kukri and tapped the log. A motley collection of small, strange creatures scuttled out and skidded away across the wet mud.

'They're only insects,' I said. I was disappointed. I expected something much more interesting, like a rat, or even a snake.

'Insects can be very dangerous. Particularly this one.' With the flat blade of her kukri, she was now holding down the largest centipede I had ever seen. It was bright red, about nine inches long, as thick as my finger and seemed to have a million legs.

'What is that?' I asked, moving back.

'This is what we call chella,' she explained as it struggled under her blade. 'It is only baby. But it is deadly. It can kill humans and even small elephant.'

'Well, for Christ's sake, kill it and throw it away.'

'Not at all. We will use for medicine.' She shouted at one of the boys to fetch her little metal tongs. She picked up the centipede carefully with the tongs and put it into an empty beer bottle, sealing the top with a plug of grass.

'We will fill bottle with mustard oil. We will allow insect to dissolve naturally. We will then use it on our bodies, to cure aches and pains.'

Aditya had joined us. He stood under an umbrella, watching with interest.

'Parbati is right you know, Mark. In Greece they use the scorpion as a similar antidote.'

I was seriously impressed by the Maratha's knowledge. 'Really? Have you ever been to Greece?'

'No,' he replied. 'I read about it the other day in Gerald Durrell's *My Family and Other Animals*.'

Considering the conditions, Parbati produced an extraordinary feast. We dined sumptuously in the openings of our wet lairs on a kind of kedgeree made from rice, potatoes, chillis and wild courgettes.

Parbati imparted one more gem of jungle law as she watched me begin to close the front of our tent.

'Your tents are full of holes now. Better to keep flap open, like me. Snakes and centipedes are only dangerous if they feel trapped.'

I had already stuffed the holes with bits of clothing. Ignoring Parbati's instructions, I closed the flap firmly. I was not taking any risks. Although the chella was now floating in mustard oil, it was, after all, only a baby. Where, I wondered, were its parents? Phandika had informed me with some glee, that adult chellas were at least eighteen inches long, fat as a sausage, and capable of killing a fully grown elephant.

Indra, mighty god of the heavens, continued to vent his wrath on us during the night as he rode across the sky, his magnificent white elephant, Airavat, trumpeting thunderously as it sent bolts of lightning down its four huge tusks.

An elephant of a more mortal kind had visited us in the night, judging by the tracks and droppings surrounding our tents in the morning. Parbati quickly checked on Kanchen.

'Well?' I asked. 'What do you think?'

She raised an eyebrow. 'Kanchen look happy. Who knows?'

I squatted down beside Parbati as she studied the deep, round imprints that lay like large puddles around our tents. 'Big elephant,' she said, 'maybe eight and half, nine feet at shoulder. He stopped for minute here.'

I shuddered. This was all getting to be too much for me. First, the killer centipede, now this. God knows what next.

Parbati laughed at my expression. 'Often during mela shikar in jungle, elephants used to come into camp. One time during rains, we were all sleeping in line on veranda of old broken bungalow. In middle of night, I feel my shawl pulled slowly off me. Sleepily, I pulled back. Quickly, it was taken from my hand. I took my kukri and look up.' She paused for a moment and grinned. 'There was big elephant standing outside veranda, holding my shawl.'

'What did you do?'

'Nothing. Why?' she shrugged, puzzled. 'It is his jungle so I let him take shawl.'

The rain continued relentlessly for the next few days. Confined to the wet and stinking canvas of my tent, I found myself becoming more and more irritable and unable to concentrate on anything. I should, I knew, have savoured every damp moment. In a week or so I would be confined again in the belly of the aircraft taking me home. But what was more irritating was that everyone else managed to keep busy – Parbati sharpening her kukri; Phandika and Dino making running repairs on the guddas; the boys, playing cards. Even Aditya occupied himself as he lay snug and cocooned in the cosy glow of the frog, now anchored by large rocks. He was working his way through his library.

But at least I had the elephants. They never failed to entertain. Lakhi became the star of the daily show. First she would roll around deliriously in the mud and apply her cosmetics. Then she would perform a kind of rhumba as she scratched her enormous backside up and down against a tree. As a finale she would toboggan into the deep nullah, pick up a log and chew on it happily, like a big fat cigar.

At long last the weather cleared and the sun came out. We struck camp. My gloom lifted as we got back on our elephants.

We traversed a switchback of hills, which rose up to form the icy white fortress of the Eastern Himalayas, silent and forbidding, guarding the lofty hermit kingdom of Bhutan. In the distance, we could hear the roar of a river, which became louder and louder as we approached.

'Rydak,' Parbati announced over the noise of the water. 'She is fast river. We will camp there tonight. Then we will ride to meet her sister, river Sankos. It is border of Assam. There, I am sorry, we must end journey. But we will have big celebration,' she added. 'We will be arriving on day of *Magh Bihu*, our harvest festival.'

I forced a smile on to my face. I had no idea we were that close to the end of our journey. Parbati leant across and punched me lightly on the arm.

'Hey, chela, cheer up. Guru will not let you down. Tomorrow I have arranged special surprise. We go to Assam. Not with elephants. I am sorry. By jeep. I am taking you to my family home in Gauripur. I think you will find it interesting. Many things of my father are there.'

I was deeply touched. Parbati was paying me a great honour by welcoming me to her home. I was also tantalised and excited. She was allowing me a glimpse of the greatest elephant guru, her father Laljee Barua, whose presence had somehow always been there, just below the surface, guiding and controlling the destiny of our journey.

*

On the banks of the Rydak, the second fastest flowing river in India, Aditya and the boys had set up camp in a small patch of forest. Phandika was delighted. It was here he had once caught eleven elephants in ten days. It was like fishing, he told us.

Aditya and I needed all our courage, and that of Lord Shiva as well, as we stood shivering, stark naked, on the riverbank, gazing down at the icy torrent that raged below us. Aditya had insisted on this act of masochism. Tonight we had planned a surprise visit to his young nephew who had just started work on a nearby tea estate.

'Got to be spick and span,' Aditya shouted at me, his teeth chattering. 'The boy's just started. A visit from his famous uncle will give him some standing in the place.'

'If I stand here much longer, I'll die!' I shouted back.

'Let's go for it!' he yelled.

Holding hands, and evoking the name of the great Lord Shiva, we plunged into the river like a pair of pansies.

An hour later, when our numbed bodies had finally thawed, we put on our best clothes. Aditya's taste was particularly sartorial. He wore neatly-pressed blue jeans, a kind of bring-em-back-alive khaki safari shirt, clean white socks and polished loafers.

'A good impression, that's the ticket,' he informed me, patting his cheeks with cologne.

Parbati hardly recognised us. 'Are you sure you are seeing your nephew?' she asked, raising her eyebrows. 'Maybe it's not good idea for you to go tonight. We have long drive tomorrow.'

'The tea estate's just next door,' Aditya replied. 'Why? Are you worried?'

'Noooo . . . but mischief has habit of following you around.'

'Baini, Parbati, baini,' Aditya reassured her, patting her on the shoulder. 'We'll be back in a jiffy.'

If only I had listened to her.

It started well enough. We arrived at the tea estate. Unfortunately, it was the wrong one. I watched with mounting apprehension as Aditya and the driver listened to a labourer as he gave instructions, flinging his arms around like a windmill in a hurricane.

'Are you sure this is the right way?' I asked Aditya anxiously as we sped down a grassy track.

'Absolutely.'

We were suddenly thrown forward as the driver hit his brakes. In front of us lay a forty foot drop into a ravine.

'Can't understand it,' said Aditya, puzzled. 'This is exactly where he told us to go.'

I sighed. I had learnt from previous experience that it is fatal to ask directions in rural India, or anywhere for that matter in this subcontinent. Not that people deliberately mislead you; they are simply more interested in having a chat. Added to this, for such a seasoned traveller, Aditya possessed no sense of direction. I could see I was in for a long night.

I settled back and dozed off. I was rudely awakened as the driver slammed on his brakes again. Either I was dreaming or the driver had taken a short cut through the Himalayas. A pair of skiers, bodies hunched forward, hurtled down a steep icy piste towards me as I peered through the windscreen of the jeep.

'Christ, that's all we need!' Aditya exclaimed angrily. 'It's the weekly film show for the labourers.'

A carpet of people blocked the road leading to the tea estate, their eyes glued to the images that flicked eerily across an immense screen hovering above us.

The driver leant on his horn. Aditya stopped him. 'A herd of elephants won't shift this lot,' he muttered.

'It's a great film,' I said, now enjoying the action. 'James Bond . . . There's a very pretty . . .'

'We have not come to the movies, Mark, we've come to see my nephew,' Aditya interrupted. 'I'll just have to find another way in.'

We reversed and turned into the road that circled the estate. After driving for a few minutes, Aditya noticed a hole in the perimeter fence.

'We'll go in there and cut across the tea gardens.'

'Are you sure that's a good idea?' I asked. It was late. A plump yellow moon sagged through some wispy clouds.

'No problem. Look, you can see the lights over there.'

Aditya told the driver to take a sharp left turn. For the third time that evening we were all thrown forward as the vehicle plunged into a deep nullah. Cursing, we struggled out and surveyed the damage. The vehicle lay up-ended, its bonnet buried like an arrow in the ditch. We looked about us nervously. In daylight, a tea garden is safe, sterile and suburban. At night, it is downright spooky, silent as a graveyard.

Aditya announced, 'We'll just have to walk and get help. It's not far.'

Leaving the terrified driver locked in the vehicle, we set off, guided by the weak beams of our torches. I looked at my watch. It was nearly ten o'clock.

'Just next door,' I muttered.

'Relax, my friend. You should be used to this. It's an adventure.'

I noticed that the limping had now been replaced by the familiar loping gait of the Maratha as we crossed the ankle-deep wet grass and turned into another avenue. I grabbed Aditya and pulled him to the ground.

'What the . . .'

'There's an elephant,' I whispered urgently into his ear. 'It's standing about a hundred and fifty yards down the avenue.'

Aditya bobbed his head up.

'Nonsense, that's one of those mobile crèches.'

I gripped him tighter.

'Since when have mobile crèches developed appetites?' We both heard the sharp crack of a branch being torn from a tree. Aditya took a quick look.

'My goodness, you're right. What do we do?'

'Don't know.'

'Well, you're supposed to be the elephant expert,' he whispered in panic. 'Think of something.'

'We could climb a tree.'

'Oh, brilliant. That'll just alert him and then he'll pull it down.'

'We could make a run for it.'

'That's even more brilliant. I can hardly run.'

'Then we'll crawl through the tea bushes.'

Aditya's eyes rounded in horror. 'You've got to be joking. There are snakes.'

'Okay,' I whispered, 'we'll just have to sit tight and hope we're down wind.'

Something moved against my foot. I jerked back and switched on the torch. A large, green and black frog blinked and then croaked.

'Rana Tigrena,' said Aditya, 'the tribals actually marry them to bring rain. It's a full wedding with . . .'

'For Christ's sake, shut up,' I hissed, punching his arm.

It was not the time or place to receive a long oration on tribal customs.

'Okay, okay, take it easy, it's just an old jungle warfare technique used by my ancestors – to keep you cool when facing danger.'

It had now begun to rain. We sat waiting for another fifteen minutes, crouched, soaked and freezing, occasionally daring to look up to check on the elephant's movements. Eventually it ambled away and disappeared into the mist.

'Okay, let's go for it,' Aditya said, and using the tea bushes as cover, we stumbled along the avenues until we reached a road. Ahead of us, a long drive led up to a large colonial bungalow.

'Well, thank God that's over,' Aditya said breathlessly. 'I bet that's the manager's house. We'll get help there.'

We walked up the drive. Aditya banged on the iron grilles. It was pitch dark inside.

'Anyone home?' he shouted.

A light came on and moved towards us. From behind the grilles a tousled chowkidar eyed us suspiciously. In one hand he held a lamp, in the other a shot-gun. Aditya explained our predicament. Reluctantly he lowered the gun and informed us that the manager was away in Calcutta, but if we followed the road for two kilometres, we would find the assistant manager's house.

'Two kilometres,' Aditya said wearily. 'I'll never make it. My leg's in agony.'

'Ask him if we can borrow that bicycle?' I said, pointing to the one leaning against the wall of the empty garage.

'I can't ride a bicycle.'

'I can. Sit on the handlebars.'

After further negotiations, we set off wobbling into the rain and mist.

By the time we arrived at the assistant manager's house, it was gone midnight. A large sign hung on the wall – 'Beware of the Dog'.

'Don't worry,' Aditya said, 'just follow my instructions.'

We carefully opened the gate. Immediately, a dog started to bark – not exactly a bark, more a deep, low roar – which increased in volume as an animal the size of a small pony rushed towards us.

I turned to flee, but Aditya stopped me.

'Just freeze and hold your hands in the air. Old Maratha technique.'

'Rambo,' a voice bellowed from the dark, 'down . . . down.'

A large Dobermann skidded to a halt just in front of us and lay down, salivating. I exhaled slowly. A tall turbaned Sikh approached us, his eyes registering both suspicion and surprise. It was the assistant manager. I did not blame him. We must have looked extraordinary – soaking wet and covered in mud. Aditya, for the second time that evening, politely explained our predicament.

'You are very lucky,' the assistant manager said. 'An old elephant has been hanging around the tea gardens. He has been wounded by villagers. He's already killed two of my labourers.' The man drove us in his jeep to Aditya's nephew's house, where the door was opened by a sleepy youngster, hastily tying a lungi around his waist.

'Randeep. You have some visitors. One of them says he is a relation of yours.'

Randeep blinked, hardly recognising his own flesh and blood.

'Errr . . . yes sir,' he stuttered, 'he is my uncle. I'm very sorry to have disturbed you.'

'Well, goodnight then. And Randeep, make sure you send somebody to fetch their vehicle. It is stuck in a nullah somewhere in the garden.'

'So much for good impressions, I remarked, as the nephew ushered us in.

The moment the door closed, judging by the respectful and then tumultuous welcome that Aditya received from everyone in the house who streamed out to greet us, it was apparent that they were not only unfazed but delighted by the head of the family's untimely arrival. I suspected that this sort of thing might have happened before.

However, like me, Randeep clearly mistrusted his uncle's sense of direction. He insisted on driving us home, closely followed by our vehicle which had by now been extracted from the nullah.

In the early hours of the morning we crept back into the camp. We were so silent, we did not even wake the mahouts, let alone the elephants, who were lying stretched out and snoring. As we eased into our tents, a voice pierced the darkness.

'Is that your jiffy? Bloody humbugs.'

17
The Shrine

We climbed into the jeep and set off on the long drive to Parbati's family home. Parbati looked especially radiant in a traditional golden silk mekla, her shoulders draped in a beautiful white shawl. I noticed she was wearing a ring I had not seen before – a tiny, bright blue sapphire set in gold.

She laughed. 'I wear this because I will be seeing Mother. Some weeks back I received letter from her. She told me, be careful. My stars are not good until March. Wear blue sapphire, you will be safe, she says. She is very superstitious.'

'When were you born, Parbati?' I asked.

She frowned. 'Is it polite to ask lady her age?'

'No, no, I'm sorry, I didn't mean that,' I explained. 'I just wanted to check your birth sign. I had a bet with myself when I first met you.'

'And . . .?'

'I think you were born in late May or June. You're a Gemini.'

She clapped her hands together in delight.

'Correct. How did you know?'

'Well,' I hesitated, 'Geminis are very lively people. And also, how can I put it, very . . .'

'. . . changing perhaps?' she asked innocently, 'like two different people?'

'That's right. The sign of Gemini represents the twins.'

'Is that good or bad, Mark?'

'Very good. My wife's a Gemini.'

'Then I am happy. Next time you come, you will bring her. She will be my girlfriend. I do not have any girl as friend.'

We stopped for a moment at a checkpoint where our papers were inspected. The officer waved us through.

'Now we are in Assam,' Parbati announced proudly. 'Welcome to my state.'

As we drove further the countryside became flatter and marshy, criss-crossed by little rivers. Bamboo grew luxuriantly in large groves.

'In my grandfather's time, all this was family estate. Fifty-five square miles in total. Big thick jungle. Even in my papa's time, there was good forest. And,' she continued as we approached a small village, 'he caught many elephants here, particularly in this area.'

I gazed in astonishment at a little road sign. The village was called Toofan.

Toofan? Toofan? I puzzled. Where had I heard that name? It was so familiar. Of course, I thought, and slapped my head. It was part of Tara's old name. When I bought her from the sadhus, she was called *Toofan Champa* – storm wind. No, I thought, it could not be. It's just a coincidence.

But it was not. The very next village we passed through was called Champa.

'Parbati,' I said slowly, 'you did say that your father caught elephants in these areas?'

'Yes, Mark. Why? Are you all right? You look like you see ghost.'

'Parbati,' I said, barely able to control my excitement, 'where did your father used to sell his elephants?'

'Papa's elephants went only to best places. There were many people who caught elephants. For them, it was just money. Catch them. Train them cruelly in maybe six days, then sell them quickly at small markets or straight to elephant merchants. Such elephants can become dangerous. Such people do not love elephants like my papa. He always spent six months training our elephants. Not by force. By love, patience and friendship. Then, when Papa thought they were ready, he would sell. Some to royal family in Bhutan. Some to royal family in Cooch Behar and other princely states. Others he would take to Sonepur, the best elephant market.'

'You did say Sonepur?'

'Yes, of course. Many elephants Papa sold there. Why?'

'Parbati,' I held my breath, 'did your father always give names to the elephants he caught?'

'Of course. What is elephant without name.'

I had to be sure. 'How would he choose names for the elephants?'

She shrugged. 'Many different reasons. Pratap Singh I think my father named after famous Assamese king, because Pratap was king of elephants. Some were named after places where they were caught and many other things. Why you asking me this?' she said, puzzled. 'You are like detective.'

Excitedly, I told her Tara's original name.

'It is possible, Mark,' she said, a smile flitting across her face, 'from your book and from what you told me, I see Tara is good, well-trained elephant. Also, she is right age. But it is difficult to know. Let us believe then' – she patted my arm – 'Tara was one of Papa's elephants. It is how it should be.'

I did not just believe, I knew it. I remembered that day at the Sonepur Mela, the day we had arrived. And I remembered Tara's weary and resigned look, how I had felt she had been there before.

Late at night we entered Gauripur. Even before we reached the house, the omnipresence of Parbati's father was apparent. We passed a small building with a sign announcing 'Pratap Singh Hospital'. It was founded by Laljee Barua in honour of his beloved elephant.

Leaving the town behind us, we drove up a steep, tree-lined avenue. The air seemed fresher. The wind sighed, as if in welcome, rustling the leaves in the trees that surrounded us. We could see the lights of the town twinkling far below. The house loomed out of the darkness, its secrets illuminated by the glow of oil lamps.

'Now we have power cuts,' said Parbati. 'My papa would have approved. He did not like electricity.'

We entered a small stone hall. Parbati picked up a flickering lamp and brightened the flame. The massive skull of an elephant stared vacantly from a corner, its empty eye-sockets veiled in cobwebs.

'That is head of Jung Bahadur, one of our elephants. At one time he was biggest in all India. Over ten feet at shoulder. But my father did not like him.'

'Why not?' I asked.

'Because he was bigger than Pratap Singh.'

We climbed a wide wooden staircase, ornately balustraded in wrought iron, leading up to a long spacious veranda. At the top of the stairs, a small bespectacled woman waited, holding a lamp. Parbati quickly touched her feet in respect and then flung her arms around her mother.

Parbati's mother folded her hands together in greeting and smiled at me, her small brown eyes glittering behind her lenses.

'See,' Parbati said, standing behind her, 'she is smaller than me.'

Parbati's mother said something. Parbati laughed. 'My mother's English is not good. She is embarrassed to speak, but she says welcome to Matiabagh. That is name of our house. It means mud garden. My grandfather built it eighty years ago. Not just this home, but whole hill, from mud. All this area is flat. This is only high point.'

Drawn by some strange force, I moved towards a door. Parbati stopped me.

'You are excited,' she said, 'but you must wait. Tomorrow I will show you all.'

*

I woke early. Impatient to explore, I tiptoed out on to the wide veranda. The sun was just beginning to gild the morning sky, its rays slowly drawing back the veils of mist that shrouded the world below me. Disturbed from the solace of their jungle eyrie by the hum of traffic as Gauripur awakened, parakeets flashed among the trees and white-bellied drongos dipped and darted through the air in pursuit of their breakfast of winged insects. The branch of a tree bent then sprang upwards as a monkey launched itself through the air and landed agilely on the balcony. He glared at me, chattering. Moving his bushy eyebrows up and down, he held out his hand. I found a half-eaten sweet in my pocket and offered it to him. He tore it out of my hand, studied it suspiciously, smelt it and then threw it over the veranda. Clearly he was used to a more sumptuous breakfast. This was Budha – or old man – Matiabagh Palace's resident monkey.

Parbati had told me the monkey's sad story the previous night. He had had a mate once and lived with her happily on the outskirts of the town. Over the years the town had encroached on the monkeys' territory and they were forced to scavenge. Tormented and stoned by youths, the monkeys had retaliated and Budha's mate had bitten a child. In revenge the locals had killed her. Budha escaped and now took refuge here, like an old sadhu serving his penance, receiving his alms from Parbati's family.

I wandered down the veranda, breathing in the cool morning air which, as the sun seeped in and warmed the bones of the old house, was now mingled with something else – something familiar. I breathed in again, deeply. It was the unmistakable and evocative smell of a pilkhana.

I walked down the staircase, under a gallery of trophy heads immortalising Laljee's old shikari days. Due to the enormous cost of upkeep, the house, like many old palaces in India, had seen better days. But its character was still indelibly stamped on its worn and eccentric facade. I wandered out into the garden. Under the spreading bower of a tree lay a stone mausoleum. Its sheer size suggested its importance. I sat and puzzled over the occupant of this magnificent tomb. The riddle was solved by the silent arrival of Parbati. She was carrying a small offering of incense and flowers which she placed at the head of the tomb.

'This,' she said quietly, 'is grave of Pratap Singh. He died in the forests many many miles away, but my father carried his heart to bury it here. He never really recovered from Pratap's death. Every day he would sit in study' – she looked towards a multi-facaded atrium, its long windows still shuttered – 'and gaze down at this grave. Every day he would bring fresh offerings. But he is gone and we continue his wishes. Now perhaps you understand how much he loved Pratap.'

We walked to the edge of the property. Below us a grove of

trees swept down to a small river which snaked around the base of the hill.

She pointed to a thicket of trees which encircled the hill. 'Down there was our pilkhana. At one time there were over fifty elephants here. Some of these trees are special kind for treating elephants, grown from cuttings collected in jungle. It was not only pilkhana, it was also hospital. All our elephants were healthy except' – she added sadly – 'Pratap.'

'What happened to him?'

'Anthrax,' she said bitterly. 'Pratap caught it from cattle. Even then jungle was full of cattle. Illegally grazing, spreading disease. Pratap was so young – just thirty-five.'

We walked back to the house and along the veranda towards a door. Parbati opened it and I followed her into a small room. It was dark inside. She went to the windows and pulled back the shutters.

'My father's study. We keep it exactly as he left it.'

I looked around in wonder at this treasure trove amassed from a life spent in the company of elephants. Now it was a shrine, proudly and lovingly preserved, in honour of Parbati's father.

'I will leave you,' she said and quickly closed the door.

I sensed Parbati's sadness. Confined in the four walls of this small sanctuary, there were just too many memories.

For a moment, I stood dazed, like a child in a toy shop. Then I began to explore.

Reverently displayed on a baize-covered table was a selection of exquisite ceremonial ankushes, some simple – forged from polished iron and brass – others more elaborate, their shafts glossily enamelled and inlaid with tiny shards of lapis-lazuli, cornelian and mother-of-pearl. On shelves, beside their wooden scabbards, decorated like Parbati's with elephants, flowers and trees lay Laljee's kukris, their long heavy blades oiled and still wickedly sharp.

Across the skin of a python draped over a wooden dresser, a little herd of carved elephants, holding onto each other's tails, trooped around a silver effigy of a dancing Ganesh, garlanded by a necklace of scented sandalwood beads.

On the windowsill I fingered a careful arrangement of whimsical knick-knacks, no doubt picked up from the forest floor over the years – a fragment of yellowing skull, a fossilised fish, sets of elephant molars, glittering rocks, shells, bundles of iridescent feathers and a gnarled root shaped like an elephant's head.

Yet it was the photographs which evoked the most potent memories. For here, hanging on the wall or propped up in frames, and lying under the glass top of a beautiful mahogany desk, was a pictorial narrative of this extraordinary man's obsession and devotion to the animal that had forged his life's destiny.

The room was dominated by one photograph – a larger version of the image Parbati had shown me in the forest lodge at Jaldapara, of her father astride his beloved elephant. Pratap Singh, in full musth, was hurling that leopard contemptuously into the air.

Others showed Laljee Barua in his mela shikar camps, dressed in a simple dhoti, surrounded by his family, and there was one of Parbati as a tiny tot, sitting on his knee, and another showing Parbati a little older, her fierce black eyes burning proudly as she perched on Pratap Singh's head.

Then there were pictures of more elephants; wild elephants in the stockade, wild elephants being trained, elephants bathing, elephants feeding in the pilkhana, ceremonial elephants, bejewelled and caparisoned standing in long lines, all dwarfed by the mighty Jung Bahadur.

I found only one photograph that seemed out of place – Laljee Barua standing outside the gates of Buckingham Palace, looking ill at ease in a suit.

Locked inside a long glass-fronted bureau lay the jewels of this little museum – Laljee's library – a priceless harvest of traditional and practical knowledge. Here, among obscure and ancient Sanskrit treatises, large leather-bound game books, diaries and bulging notebooks, I knew I would unveil many secrets – for me the most important perhaps was a record of the capture of a beautiful female elephant named Toofan Champa.

I reached out to turn the key, but something stopped me. I

felt I would be intruding. This was a personal legacy. However privileged, I was still only a guest.

Parbati came to collect me. On the ground floor of the house, she unlocked an old door. It groaned in protest as we tried to force it open. It gave all of a sudden, and a cloud of dust seeped out slowly, like gas escaping from the broken seals of an Egyptian tomb. My nostrils twitched and I shivered. I had discovered the source of that unmistakable smell of a pilkhana that had lightly scented the old house earlier that morning.

It was dark inside. Parbati handed me a torch.

'This used to be billiard room. Now it is storeroom of my papa's things from jungle camps. I do not like to go in there. There are spiders.'

It was a weak excuse for someone like Parbati; grief for her father might overwhelm her.

Guided by the weak beam of the torch, I stepped inside, pushing away the cobwebs that criss-crossed the room like empty hammocks. In a corner, I disturbed a family of mice, resting in a pile of rotting guddas, which were stacked like hay bales and still tainted after all these years with the sweat marks from the backs of elephants.

Under a jumble of gun-cases, picnic hampers and leather ammunition boxes I pulled out an old ceremonial howdah, its silver casing blackened with age, its once plush red velvet seat now faded and frayed.

Curious, I lifted the cover off the billiard table. A cloud of mosquitos erupted from the mouldy green baize, on which lay fishing rods, rattan baskets, clusters of hand-forged hooks and an old cane solar topee.

A glint of metal revealed a cornucopia of large brass cooking bowls, a poignant reminder of the scale of the old Shikar camps set up deep in the forests, where guests would be served in splendour by a retinue of servants.

Rows of moth-eaten heads of leopard and tiger glared down at me from the walls. I tripped on the barrels of a pile of ancient muskets and fell into the embrace of a stuffed black bear. Entwined, we toppled slowly backwards into the battered chassis of a jeep. I scrambled to my feet, feeling nervous. It was as if I had awakened the ghosts that had lain dormant for so many years. Closing the door firmly behind me, I returned upstairs, drawn to the security of Laljee's study.

The afternoon sun streamed in through the big windows, bright, warm and reassuring. I sat down in Laljee's chair and imagined him sitting here, gazing out on his beloved elephant's grave, listening, not to the hum of traffic, now filtering upwards, but to the sounds of his elephants in the pilkhana below. In his last years, he was interviewed about his life's work for a book. He had said:

I have honourably retreated from the struggle for existence and made my life in the forests. I have not been able to keep pace with the progress of society and life, so I have found my resting place in the calm shades of the forest. I have become, as it were, a special kind of wild animal. I do not regret that. What I have seen and received from living in the forest cannot be compared with anything else. I have however, a small fear. Will there be at least a small forest area and a small piece of shade left in the long run, where I shall be able to stretch my limbs in peace?

Perhaps, surrounded by everything he loved, he had found it here. As we left I noticed a small sign on the door.
'P. C. Barua – IN'.
For me he had never left.

18
Mahout's Lament

I awoke with an uneasy feeling in my stomach, a feeling that as a boy recalled the dread of returning to school. It had been late by the time we had reached camp and I had fallen into a deep sleep. Now outside my tent I could hear Phandika whistling cheerfully, the elephants feeding noisily and the murmur of the boys above the clatter of pots and pans. For them it was just another day. For me it was my last with my guru.

'Hurry up, Mark,' a familiar voice cut through my gloom. 'Sun is rising.'

We saddled up the elephants and I swung up on to Kanchen's back for the last time. I pushed my feet into the stirrups and waited, but Phandika did not join me. I turned to Parbati, who was sitting alone on Lakhi's back.

'Where's Phandika?'

'Phandika and Dino are going in jeep. We talked late last night while you were sleeping. We all decided together, you are at last worthy of Kanchen. She is yours. Chalo, brother mahout!'

Brother Mahout. I savoured the words in my mind. It had taken three months. That first day Parbati had said it could take five years. Then I realised she was right. It had indeed taken five years.

What had started as a whim with Tara, in the lush jungles of eastern India, had now finally been fulfilled in a remote patch of forest in the shadow of the mighty Himalayas. The distance geographically was not great; the distance in time enormous. My apprenticeship was finally over, and with great pride I dug my toes behind Kanchen's ears and followed my guru through the morning mist across the wide reaches of the river Rydak.

As with all people who have travelled together and shared the hardships and difficulties of life on the road, Parbati and I shared an easy familiarity and we rode, side by side, comfortable in our silence. I would have preferred to have ridden through a more peaceful and optimistic environment as our journey drew to an end, but Parbati, true to her character both as guide and guru, had never pulled punches. She had shown me clearly and sometimes ghoulishly just how bleak the future was for these beautiful animals, and this was perhaps a final and ominous testimonial.

Our passage was impeded by the mass of humanity and livestock that moved inexorably below us. Lakhi suddenly swerved, alarmed by the unexpected and hideous whine of an accelerating motorcycle as it swept past perilously close to her legs. Cursing, Parbati was forced for the first time in two months to use her little ankushes and quickly brought Lakhi under control.

We cut off the road on to a narrow track bordered by forest on either side, from which spilled a stream of cattle and goats. As we approached they scattered in terror, their neck-bells jangling in a discordant cacophony. Groups of men, women, and even children, their backs bent under heavy loads of timber, gazed up as we passed.

'Elephants in these areas are doomed,' Parbati said. 'I pray our film can be lesson. We *must* protect what is left of them. Protect them like jewels. People do not understand. Elephants are important for *our* survival. By saving them we are forced to save big forests. By saving big forests we save all animals. If we do not, all nature will disappear and' – she shrugged – 'we destroy ourselves.'

She sighed. 'I will fight on. I cannot live without elephants. Whatever happens, for rest of my life I will always keep them with me. They teach you so much.'

Parbati was right. One cannot expect to save all the elephants. But if Parbati and people like her are given support, their experience respected and utilised, then there is some hope; for they are custodians of ancient elephant lore, a treasury of traditional knowledge and practical skills which have been passed down over the centuries and are a lifeline to the conservation, better understanding and the future of these magnificent animals.

In the early afternoon we skirted the perimeter of a tea estate and crossed a wide scrubby plateau that fell away neatly, as if cut like a cake by the smooth and swollen expanse of water that flowed beneath us.

After two months on the road, our travels were to end here, on the banks of the river Sankos, which demarcated the border between Bengal and Assam.

*

At the camp, I reluctantly dismounted from Kanchen for the last time and watched her fondly as she was led away by Phandika to join Dino and Lakhi in the river for a long and well-earned bath.

All around us, the villagers were preparing for the harvest festival of *Magh Bihu*, tending to the bonfires that symbolised the fulfilment of the season's hard labour, and around which they would dance, sing, drink and make merry throughout the night.

Judging by the scale of our bonfire and the amount of liquor, Parbati had ensured that we too were going to celebrate, in fitting style, not only the harvest festival but the end of our journey.

And that was not to be all. For soon we were joined by one of India's greatest folk singers, Pratima Pandey, whose extraordinary talent had gained her India's highest cultural award. Not only was she a national treasure, she was also Parbati's sister.

She was accompanied by three musicians, their instruments simple, but beautiful – a large *dhol* or drum; a *sarinda*, a two-stringed wooden violin fashioned like a smiling elephant stretching out its trunk; and a *dotara*, a kind of small sitar, its gourd-shaped base carved with flowers and covered with the mottled skin of a monitor lizard.

A smile spread across Pratima's worn but proud face. 'My instruments have no glamour. They are rough. But they are my children, and this,' she added, raising a full glass of rum to her lips, 'this is our magic.'

Laljee Barua's daughter Pratima, like Parbati, had grown up steeped in elephant lore. The themes of her songs celebrated this world – the catching and training of wild elephants, the nomadic life of the mahouts, and the lament and longing of loved ones left behind.

The musicians began to play. Tapping a cluster of small brass bells against her knee, Pratima lifted her face to the sky and sang:

> Mahout! The jungle is very dangerous.
> Snakes will bite you, scorpions sting you.
> The healer will chant mantras for the poison
> Brushing your wounds with his ferns.
>
> Come to me, O fearless mahout
> Turn your elephant towards my door.
> I will suck out the poison
> I will brush your wound with my hair.

Her voice, at first low and soft as the fall of fine rain, began to soar effortlessly and then, like a bird caught by the wind, hovered for a moment and was gently swept away, echoing into the distance.

> O my mahout on a tusker.
> Can a boat sail in a lake without water?
> What can a woman do with her beauty
> If her mahout is no longer near her?
>
> O my mahout on a tusker.
> I left my mother and my brother
> I left my golden home
> And now you have left me, weeping.
>
> O heartless mahout on a tusker.

I sat listening, transfixed by the magic of the music in the deepening dusk. Behind us, Lakhi and Kanchen were playing, their trunks entwined. I caught myself thinking of Tara, wishing she had a companion to share her palatial home.

Now the drummer was using the heels of his hands to produce

a deeper beat under the singer's voice.

> I tie the wild elephant front and back.
> I cannot bind his pride.
> Calling the name of Hari
> I take my seat and ride.

> The death lizard calls five times overhead.
> Five times the sand bird cries.
> I married but left my young wife behind.
> Who will mourn this mahout if he dies?

> In the dark forest wild elephants hide.
> A mahout fell, was trampled and died.
> I tighten the rope that cuts my feet.
> In the name of Hari I ride.

Phandika was sitting quietly on Kanchen, his eyes closed, tears running down his old, weather-beaten face as the words of the songs spun through the cobwebs of his mind, evoking memories of a past and golden time.

The sun dipped below the horizon. Pratima and Parbati climbed on to Lakhi's back and embraced. Serenaded by the musicians below, the sisters sang together in praise of the great animal that had forged the destiny of their family.

*

Late that night, after our celebrations had ended and her sister had left, Parbati performed a small puja to initiate me as a mahout. In the flickering light of our dying bonfire, I bowed down before her three times and received her blessing. Following tradition, I showed my respect by presenting my guru with gifts of alcohol, an item of clothing, chickens and money. In return she handed me the basic requirements of a mahout – a gunny bag, a kukri and a pair of metal tongs.

Then, from a small cloth bag, she took out a metal bracelet, its two ends fashioned as elephant heads.

'I have blessed this for you at my temple. Always keep it near you. It will be lucky.'

She placed it around my wrist. 'When I became mahout I also receive something special from my guru. It is lucky for me. My papa gave me this.' She picked up the little brass vessel that had intrigued me for so long. It was then that Parbati revealed at last the secret of her kamandalu.

Once upon a time, she began, a Brahmin and his wife lived happily in a small shack on the banks of the river Dnoa-sia (the river of Divine Illusion or Miracle) near Gauripur in the foothills of Bhutan. One fateful day the Brahmin arrived home with a new wife. Although she was ugly and vain, he had succumbed to her family's wealth. Before long the Brahmin had built a splendid new house which humbled his former dwelling. The couple were attended by a retinue of servants and soon he had almost forgotten his first wife who spent her days alone, crying her heart out in the little shack next door. The young wife was, however, given one menial chore – she was allowed to collect water from the river in a big golden vessel and carry it home on her head. So she would sit on the riverbank and cry, her tears falling into the flowing water. One day, the King of the Elephants and his subjects came to drink from this river. Wondering why the water tasted so salty, he asked his herd the reason. They told him of the young wife's misfortune. Immediately he went to find her. On hearing her tale of woe, he said mankind lacked compassion and kindness. He offered to take her to his home where she would be treated like a queen. The young wife hesitated for a moment, then, without warning, there was a violent flash flood, bursting the river's banks. A torrent swept down towards them, carrying the debris of her little shack and her cruel husband's new home. The King of the Elephants lifted her on to his back and they ran for seven days and seven nights. Finally they arrived at the Kingdom of the Elephants, high in the foothills of the Himalayas. There in his ivory palace he placed her reverently on his ivory throne and, kneeling before her, asked her to marry him. The young wife happily agreed and all the elephants trumpeted in jubilation in honour of their new queen. At the coronation, seven different coloured streams of water were poured over her and she slowly transformed into a beautiful female elephant, the golden vessel becoming her head, the spout her trunk. The elephants raised their trunks in obeisance and the King of the Elephants announced: 'Listen, O Queen, from this day on, we will obey you. Your command is final.'

'And that,' Parbati said softly, a wry smile spreading across her face as she caressed her little kamandalu, 'is how elephants became matriarchal.'

★

We broke camp early. Aditya and I had a long drive ahead to catch the aeroplane back to Delhi. We loaded our kit into the jeep, now almost empty, its former contents ingeniously arranged and strapped across the backs of the two elephants.

I fed Kanchen for the last time and stroked her face affectionately. She had been a steady and faithful companion. I would miss her. I embraced all the boys. I would miss them too. As I extracted myself from Phandika's bear-hug, during which he had lifted my last packet of cigarettes, he presented me with a small memento – the glossy tail feathers of Donald McCullin CBE.

Parbati stood alone, deadly as ever in her gunslinger's gear.

'Well, boss.'

'Well, brother mahout,' she said, pushing back those dark shades and slapping her hand down on mine. 'One day, God willing, we will continue our journey. In meantime, do not forget us, and', she warned, 'do not forget elephants.'

'You don't have to worry about that,' I replied, 'I'll be back soon.'

She climbed on to Lakhi's back.

'Yes. Your training for mahout is not yet complete.'

'But, Parbati.' I was bewildered. 'You've just made me a mahout.'

'I forget one thing.' She chuckled as she moved away. 'I do not teach you cooking. What good is mahout without cooking.'

'Parbati!' I wailed after her. 'That's not fair . . .'

My pleading was in vain. Like Pugli Sahan, the spirit of the Elephant Goddess, Parbati had mysteriously disappeared, her laughter echoing through the thick morning mist.

Epilogue

A year or so has now passed since I made that journey. Meanwhile, back in India, I learn that the elephants are fighting even more desperately for their survival.

Recently, a starving herd of sixty adults and calves were driven from their home by forest fires. They rampaged for one hundred and fifty miles across a heavily populated area, incurring fatalities on both sides. They were halted just sixty miles from Calcutta, and – burnt, battered and bewildered – driven back to find temporary refuge in yet another unstable environment.

For once news of their plight was not confined to the local media. It made the front pages worldwide in some of the major international newspapers – a poignant and perverse plea to take notice that another elephant, an elephant just as beautiful, just as majestic as the African elephant, was making that same last-ditch stand, in another part of the world, against the inexorable tide of mankind.

I often think of Parbati, sometimes unintentionally, when the trunks of the little elephant heads that form the ends of the bracelet tug reproachfully as they snag in my clothes. Then I think of that evening – our last – when Parbati presented me with this blessed and lucky talisman.

I made two wishes that night. One has already come true – the result now lies before me, her big eyes gazing up in wonder at the congregation of strange pot-bellied creatures with big ears and long noses that dance magically in the air above her cot.

And the other . . .? A few days ago I received this letter.

KIPLING CAMP

(KANHA NATIONAL PARK, M.P.)
Mail Address
C/o Tollygunge Club Ltd.
120, D.P. Sasmal Road, Calcutta-700 033

Mark Shand Esq.   20 November 1994.

My dear Mark,

It is my very real pleasure to let you know that I have just received official permission from the Government of India for your beloved Tara to be betrothed.

Her fiancé is a splendid chap – hardworking, handsome and huge. Keeping fingers crossed.

Warm personal regards.

Yours ever,

(R. H. Wright, O.B.E.)

My fingers too are firmly crossed.

Bibliography

Salim Ali, *The Book of Indian Birds*, Bombay National History Society, Bombay, 1979

W. A. J. Archbold, *Bengal Haggis: Or the Lighter Side of Indian Life*, The Scholartis Press, London, 1928

K. L. Barua Bahadur, *Early History of Kamarupa*, Shillong, Assam, 1933

B. N. Dutta Barooa, *The Red River and the Blue Hill*, Advocate Lawyer's Book Stall, Gauhati, Assam, 1954

A. L. Basham, *The Wonder that Was India*, Sidgwick & Jackson, London, 1958

William Bazé, *Just Elephants*, Elek Books, London, 1955

Robert Berkow, Andrew J. Fletcher, *The Merck Manual of Diagnosis and Therapy* (fifteenth edition), Merck Sharp & Dohme Research Laboratories, West Point PA, 1987

Panchugopal Bhattacharyaya, *Fifty Years with Elephants: a Brief Account of the Life-Long Experiences of Prince Prakitish Chandra Barua about Elephants*, Brajakishore Mandal, Calcutta, 1982 (personally translated by Sagar Choudhury)

Colonel A. Bloomgate, Indian Army, *The Plain Narrative of the doings and destruction of the Most murderous Rogue ever Known*, Saxmundham, 1895

Richard Carrington, *Elephants*, Chatto and Windus, London, 1958

Dr Pratap Chandra Choudhury (ed.), *Hastividyarnava*, Publication Board, Assam, Gauhati, 1976

Amal Kumar Das, *The Totos*, Scheduled Castes and Tribes Welfare Department, Government of Bengal, Calcutta, 1969

Amal Kumar Das and Manis Kumar Raha, 'The Rabhas of West Bengal', Government of West Bengal, Calcutta, 1967

Amal Kumar Das and Hemendra Nath Banerjee, 'Impact of Tea Industry on the Life of the Tribals of West Bengal', Government of West Bengal, Calcutta, 1964

Gayatri Devi of Jaipur and Santha Rama Rau, *A Princess Remembers: The Memories of the Maharani of Jaipur*, Weidenfeld & Nicolson, London, and J. B. Lippincot, USA, 1976

Franklin Edgerton (tr), *The Elephant-Lore of the Hindus*: 'The Elephant Sport (Matanga-Lila) of Nilakantha', Yale University Press, 1931

Sir J. Emmerson Tennant, *The Wild Elephant*, Longmans Green, London, 1867

S. K. Eltringham, *The Illustrated Encyclopedia of Elephants from their Origins and Evolution to their Ceremonial and Working Relationship with Man*, Salamander Books, London, 1991

Abu'L-Fazl, *Ain-I-Akbari* (translated by H. Blochmann), Calcutta-Asiatic Society of Bengal, Bengal, 1927

Francis and Thomas (eds), *Jataka Tales*, Jaico Publishing House, Ashwin J. Shah, Bombay, 1987

W. M. Fraser, *The Recollections of a Tea Planter*, The Tea and Rubber Mail, London, 1935

U. N. Gohain, *Assam under the Ahoms*, Jorhat, Assam, 1942

Praphulladatta Goswami, *Bihu Songs of Assam*, Lawyer's Bookstall, Gauhati, Assam, 1957

Joseph Dalton Hooker, *Himalaya Journals*, John Murray, London, 1854

Sir William Wilson Hunter, *Annals of Rural Bengal*, Smith, Elder & Co, London, 1897

Sir William Wilson Hunter, *A Statistical Account of Bengal* (volume x), Trübner & Co, London, 1876

Pradyumna P. Karan and William M. Jenkins Jnr, *The Himalayan Kingdoms*, D. Van Nostrad Inc., Princeton, New Jersey, 1963

John Lockwood Kipling CIE, *Beast and Man in India* (A popular sketch of Indian animals in their relations with the people), Macmillan, London, 1904

Jeffrey Masson and Susan McCarthy, *When Elephants Weep: The Emotional Lives of Animals*, Jonathan Cape, London, 1994

A. J. W. Milroy (Deputy Conservator of Forests, Assam), 'A Short Treatise on the Management of Elephants', Shillong: printed at the Government Press, Assam, 1922

W. Nassau-Lees, 'Memorandum Written after a Tour Through the Tea Districts of Eastern Bengal in 1864–65', Bengal Secretariat Press, Calcutta, 1866

Bruce Palling, *India, A Literary Companion*, John Murray, London 1992

Michel Peissel, *Lords and Lamas*, Heinemann, London, 1970

Bibliography

G. P. Sanderson, *Pack Gear for Elephants*, Calcutta, 1887

G. P. Sanderson, *Thirteen Years Among the Wild Beasts of India*, W. H. Allen, London, 1890

Charu Chandra Sanyal, *The Meches and the Totos: Sub-Himalayan Tribes of North Bengal*, The University of North Bengal, Darjeeling, West Bengal, 1973

Mark Shand, *Travels on My Elephant*, Jonathan Cape, London, 1991

R. A. Stein, *Tibetan Civilisation*, Faber and Faber, London, 1972

P. D. Stracey, *Elephant Gold*, Weidenfeld & Nicolson, London, 1963

P. D. Stracey, *Reade, Elephant Hunter*, Robert Hale, London, 1967

R. Sukumar, *The Asian Elephant: Ecology and Management*, Cambridge University Press, 1989

John Symington, *In a Bengal Jungle*, University of North Carolina Press, 1935

Leonardo da Vinci, *The Notebooks of Leonardo da Vinci*, arranged and translated by Edward MacCurdy, George Braziller, New York, 1954

Major L. A. Waddell, *Among the Himalayas*, Constable, London, 1899

J. H. Williams, *Elephant Bill*, Rupert Hart-Davis, London, 1950

Colonel Henry Yule and A. C. Burnell, *Hobson-Jobson*, John Murray, London, 1903

Gazeteers

West Bengal District Gazeteers – Koch Bihar, 1977

Assam District Gazeteers, volume iv – Kamrup, 1905

Gazeteer of India: West Bengal – Jalpaiguri, 1981

Imperial Gazeteer of India, provincial series volume ii – Bengal, 1909

Assam District Gazeteers – Goalpara District, 1979

Eastern Bengal and Assam, District Gazeteers – Jalpaiguri, 1911

Bengal District Gazeteers – Darjeeling, 1907

Assam District Gazeteers, volume iii – Goalpara, 1905

Bengal District Gazeteers – Darjeeling, 1947

Acknowledgments

To complete both a book and a film, I relied heavily on the generosity of so many around the world. I hope I have succeeded in thanking everyone.

Above all, I would like to thank Parbati Barua. It was her magic, dedication and friendship that made this possible.

My sincerest gratitude is due to:

In India – The Government of India; The Government of West Bengal; The Government of Assam; Shri Kamal Nath, Minister of State, Environment and Forests; Shri Hiteswar Saikia, Chief Minister of Assam; S C Dey, Chief Wildlife Warden, West Bengal; The Ministry of the Environment; The Forest Department of West Bengal; Rajmata Gayatri Devi of Jaipur; S Deb Roy; S S Bist; Tavleen Singh; Ranjit Barthakur; Toby Sinclair; Naveen Patnaik; Krupakaran David; The Goodricke Group of Companies, Calcutta; the Barua family; Pratima Pandey and musicians; Ramesh Nambiar and his team from Mountain Travels, Delhi; Jorden Norbhu and his team from Travel Slique, Darjeeling; Jeewan and Nina Pradhan and the staff of Meenglas Tea Estate; Mr Sharma, Ashok and Mamlu Chatterjee and the staff of Gandrapara Tea Estate; Harinder and Shanta Nain and the staff of Sankos Tea Estate, Manoj and Preeti Varma of Killcot Tea Garden; Randeep and Ujwala Singh of Rydak Tea Estate; Mr Bhattacharjee and the Mal Bazar Elephant Squad; Bob, Anne and Belinda Wright and the staff of Kipling Camp, Kanha National Park; Deepa Hazarika of Sheba Travels, Gauhati; Ajit Gulabchand; Bikram Grewal; Shobita Punja; Ashok Kumar; Frenny Khodaji; Durga Roy; Mr P R S Oberoi and the management and staff of the Oberoi Hotel, New Delhi; Joanna Van Gruisen; Diba Ansari, J B Singh and Ken Washington of British Airways; Amitava Dutt and the staff of the Mal Bazar Tourist Lodge; The Asian Elephant Specialist Group; and my fellow mahouts, Phandika, Dino, Poni, and Babul, who made me feel part of their world.

In Bhutan – The Royal Government of Bhutan; Lyonpo Dawa Tsering; Lyonpo Om Pradhan; Lyonpo C Dorji; Lhendup Dorji; Khendum Dorji; Chuni Dorji; Tobgyel Dorji; Tashi Tobgyel Wangdi and Chimi of Chhundu Travels and the Druk Hotel, Thimpu.

In England – The Indian High Commission; Peter Leggatt; Gopal Gandhi and the Nehru Institute; Sagar Choudhury; Angela Connor; Rajvir Kadan; Mark Rose of Fauna and Flora International; Marie-Paule Nougaret; Talitha Puri; Judith Fessler; Adrian Packer, and Jackie Tye of Marshfield Office Training Services for her impeccable typing.

From Discovery Productions – I would particularly like to thank Tim Cowling, Denise Baddour and Stacey Seidl Ray. Also, Clark Bunting, Greg Moyer, Steve Burns, Holly Stadtler, Dawn Sinsel Quattrucci, Valerie Grady, Chris Moseley, Amy Abbey, Dan Stanton, Mary Clare Baquet, Mick Kaczorowski and Patricia Petersen. I would also like to acknowledge Susan Tressler of IUCN/Species Survival Commission, Chicago Zoological Society, Brookfield, Illinois, who, with kind co-operation of the Discovery Channel, has tirelessly masterminded fund-raising for the Asian Elephant.

From Icon Films, Bristol – William Ennals, Peter Brandt, Laura House, Melanie Nieuwenhuys, Claire Featherstone and Nick Bain.

Very special thanks to the intrepid and patient film crew, who shared many an adventure: Harry Marshall, producer/director; John Bulmer, photography; Alastair Kenneil, sound recordist; Douglas Wade, assistant camera and Shernaz Italia, location co-ordinator.

I owe an enormous debt of gratitude to my editor Tony Colwell, and to Jenny Cottom at Jonathan Cape; and of course to my agent, Abner Stein.

Finally, I would like to thank Gita, Aditya and Clio – for them no acknowledgment is adequate. And last but not least my affection and gratitude to three large and very special ladies, Kanchen Mala, Lakhi Mala and of course, Tara. Without elephants, life would be a dull old place.

M.S.

Asian Elephant Appeal

The survival of the beautiful and majestic Asian elephant is critically threatened, and immediate action is needed to protect remaining populations.

Working at the forefront of Asian elephant conservation is the **Asian Elephant Specialist Group (AESG)** of **IUCN – The World Conservation Union**. Operating under the auspices of IUCN's Species Survival Commission – a volunteer network of 5,000 scientists, field researchers, government officials and conservation leaders – the AESG is comprised of 60 volunteer members from south and south-east Asia, the United Kingdom, Europe and the United States. Mark Shand serves as one of the AESG's volunteer members.

In 1990, AESG members together compiled the Asian Elephant Conservation Action Plan, a status report on the Asian elephant and an outline of conservation priorities. Implementation of the Plan is co-ordinated through the IUCN/SSC Asian Elephant Conservation Centre, housed at the Indian Institute of Science in Bangalore.

Urgent funds are needed to accelerate these priority conservation activities, in particular to help resolve human-elephant conflicts, determine geographic distribution of elephants, and to support training schools for mahouts.

Please help by making a generous donation today. Fauna and Flora International has agreed to collect funds on behalf of AESG.

Please send your cheque to:
Asian Elephant Appeal
Fauna and Flora International
1 Kensington Gore
London SW7 2AR

To make an instant credit card donation, please call
Fauna and Flora International
on Freephone 0800 132696

Fauna and Flora International, founded in 1903, is the world's oldest international conservation charity. Its mission is to safeguard the future of Endangered Species of animals and plants and it has members and/or projects in over 100 different countries around the globe.

100% of your donation will go to
conserving the Asian elephant

Thank you for your support